Years of
POVERTY
Years of
PLENTY

The Changing Economic
Fortunes of American
Workers and Families

Greg J. Duncan

with Richard D. Coe, Mary E. Corcoran, Martha S. Hill,
Saul D. Hoffman, and James N. Morgan
and a foreword by Lee Rainwater

Survey Research Center • Institute for Social Research
The University of Michigan

Library of Congress Cataloging in Publication Data:
Duncan, Greg, J.
    Years of poverty, years of plenty.

    Bibliography: p.
    Includes index.
    1. Cost and standard of living—United States—Longitudinal studies. 2. Income distribution—United States—Longitudinal studies. 3. Labor and laboring classes—United States—Longitudinal studies. I. University of Michigan. Survey Research Center. II. Title.
    HD6983.D85   1984   339.4'1'0973   83-12923
    ISBN 0-87944-285-9

ISR Code Number 4591

Published 1984 by:
Institute for Social Research,
The University of Michigan, Ann Arbor, Michigan

6 5 4 3 2 1
Manufactured in the United States of America

Foreword

This book reports the findings from a truly unique social study, the Panel Study of Income Dynamics. Every year since 1968, interviewers from the Survey Research Center of The University of Michigan have been making return visits to talk to the heads of some 5,000 American families. These respondents, whose families represent the nation as a whole, have agreed to share yearly information about their families' economic situation, their jobs, their income from various sources including governmental transfers such as unemployment or welfare, and other aspects of their lives.

One of the things that makes this study unique is that as individuals leave the original households and set up their own new households—for example, when marriages break up or grown children leave home—the study follows them also. This kind of continuity is not possible to obtain from traditional cross-sectional surveys, which take their data from interviews conducted at a single point in time.

The picture that emerges from these data is one that challenges a great deal of conventional wisdom about American life in general and about certain social groups in particular. We often take for granted the notion of a settled life and the idea that people who are now in poor, or affluent, or average circumstances are likely to have been so and to remain so for a long time. But these assumptions do not fit the complex picture that emerges when individuals' life circumstances over time are precisely defined in such terms as hourly wages, hours worked in a year, family income, or the ratio of family income to family need. In fact, while the study examines many different dimensions, the findings converge on a common theme—Americans' lives change a great deal even over the relatively short period of a decade, with many people experiencing important changes in occupational position, in income, and in labor force participation.

To date, the Panel Study researchers themselves have issued ten volumes of technically complex papers reporting an enormous wealth of findings on the economic welfare of Americans, and scholars at other institutions continue to add a growing number of other technical papers based on these Panel Study data. But the study has demanded new statistical approaches to analysis, and this new methodology is itself a challenge, making it difficult to convey these findings to a broad audience accustomed to traditional methods of obtaining and interpreting socioeconomic survey data.

In this volume, Greg J. Duncan addresses this broader audience, distilling the study's core findings for the decade from the late 1960's through the 1970's. His emphasis is on substance, reported in straightforward language. But he also summarizes the important differences between the familiar cross-sectional and the less familiar longitudinal surveys and guides the reader toward an understanding of the basic methods developed to organize and interpret this continuously growing body of data.

For example, one of the first things the analysts learned as they began to work with these data was that the commonsense category of "family"—by which we usually mean a nuclear family living together—is an extremely problematic concept when one takes a longitudinal perspective on families over time. A moment's thought reminds us that families are in fact constantly changing as time passes, and so are the circumstances and events of the external world that surrounds them.

It turns out that the only perspective that works for analyzing peoples' experiences over time is an *individual* life course perspective. An individual's sense of well-being is deeply affected by his or her family situation. This is consistent with Panel Study evidence that many individuals experience changes in the set of people with whom they live and that these changes in family composition are strongly linked to changes in individuals' economic status. In particular, the researchers found that changes in family composition (see Chapter 1) are important factors to be considered in understanding the dynamics of poverty and welfare (see Chapters 2 and 3).

We also learn from this longitudinal perspective that far more people than might be imagined are in need of a social safety net at some point in their lives: For example, between 1968 and 1978 nearly one-third of the married men experienced major unemployment, and an equal and somewhat overlapping proportion had acquired some type of disability. In the same ten years, about one-quarter of all American adults and children had lived at least one year on a poverty-level income and the proportion would have been much greater had it not been for transfer income programs such as unemployment compensation and welfare. In fact, fully one-quarter of all Americans lived in families that received welfare in at least one of those ten years.

Integrating the results of this study into our larger concepts of society requires a dual perspective on the way patterns observed for individuals' lives fit into larger patterns observed at the societal level. On the one hand, the findings attest to the frequent, seemingly random ups and downs of people's lives, but on the other, to the persistence of patterns of advantage or disadvantage affecting certain identifiable groups, as exemplified by the findings presented in Chapters 5 and 6 on the earnings of black men and of women.

The Panel Study of Income Dynamics is unique in the archives of social science. Its longitudinal perspective on a continuing sample of the American population, accumulating a detailed history over time of people's changing fortunes, permits researchers to analyze the way events and circumstances reported at one point in a person's life are related to the life events and circumstances reported by that person at a later point. Thus it provides social scientists with an unprecedented opportunity to observe the complex patterns of events and developments at individual, family, and societal levels, and to study the way these patterns affect the economic well-being of this microcosm of the American population. While its innovative methodology continues to attract growing interest among other social scientists and from government officials in other nations because of the new light it can shed on important social issues, the Panel Study of Income Dynamics remains unparalleled in the world.

Lee Rainwater
Harvard University
March 1983

Preface

The Panel Study of Income Dynamics, begun in 1968 under the direction of James N. Morgan, is conducted by the Survey Research Center of The University of Michigan. Data from this longitudinal study of American families provide the basis for the research findings reported in this book.

The Panel Study of Income Dynamics was originally funded by the Office of Economic Opportunity, and later by the Department of Health and Human Services, the National Science Foundation, the National Institute on Aging, and three private foundations: Sloan, Ford, and Rockefeller. Designed to supplement and complement the regular assessments of poverty conducted by the Bureau of the Census, the Panel Study has followed a large, representative sample of families, reinterviewing this same sample each year since 1968. It is intended to provide insights into factors affecting changes in family well-being by observing the same people over an extended period of time, collecting a mixture of economic, behavioral, and attitudinal information from them. The original design called for an atypically large fraction of low-income families, but included a complete, representative sample of families at all income levels as well. Although many of the initial analyses focused on the poor, Panel Study information has been used increasingly to analyze changes in economic status at all income levels.

The Panel Study data have been analyzed by literally hundreds of researchers around the country. The project staff itself has published its findings in ten annual volumes: *Five Thousand American Families—Patterns of Economic Progress*, Volumes 1–10. However, many of the most important findings from the study have yet to reach the larger public. This is due, in part, to the technical nature of the analysis and to the difficulties of converting research results into a nontechnical form that accurately communicates the nature of the evidence.

The findings presented here are based, for the most part, on the ten previously published analysis volumes, organized here into chapters covering six broad topic areas. Chapter 1 is an overview of findings on change in family economic well-being. Chapters 2 and 3 focus on the dynamics of two aspects of the lower end of the income distribution—poverty and receipt of welfare income. Chapters 4, 5, and 6 concern labor market phenomena: Chapter 4 presents an overview of work hours and earnings, with the emphasis on the largest group of workers, white men; the subject of Chapter 5 is the interpretation of recent trends in racial differences in labor market outcomes; and Chapter 6 focuses on the labor market differences between men and women.

As with each of the ten analysis volumes, this book represents the work of many people, and has several co-authors (listed in the Contents under each chapter). The list of references can guide the interested reader to the relevant sources in the ten analysis volumes, and to findings of other researchers using both Panel Study data and data from other longitudinal data sets. However, the reader is referred to the analysis volumes for complete bibliographic information.

This book began as a sabbatical project at Cornell University during the 1980-81 academic year and I am particularly indebted to the innumerable colleagues there who read very early versions of chapter drafts and gave me not only needed advice but also encouragement. Their assistance includes contributions from Glen Elder, Gary Fields, Jennifer Gerner, Ramona Heck, Robert Hutchens, Nicholas Kiefer, E. Scott Maynes, Olivia Mitchell, Phyllis Moen, Anne Shlay, Sharon Smith, Heather Weiss, and Cathleen Zick.

The long gestation period of the book beyond the Cornell sabbatical was nurtured by helpful suggestions from scores of colleagues at The University of Michigan and outside of it. The Michigan group includes: Sue Augustyniak, Jerald Bachman, Samuel Barnes, William Birdsall, Joan Brinser, Barbara Browne, Linda Datcher, Deborah Friedman, Edward Gramlich, F. Thomas Juster, George Katona, Jeffrey Liker, Sandra Newman, Michael Ponza, and William Zimmerman.

Those outside of Michigan include: David Ellwood, Bjorn Gustaffson, Anders Klevmarken, Jonathan Lane, Jan Leventer, Stewart Mandell, Deborah Miller, Lee Rainwater, Martin Rein, Marvin Shapiro, and Dorothy Telfer.

Barbara Browne, Anita Ernst, and Sherry Monroe provided excellent typing assistance. Toni Kennedy edited the manuscript with skill and a needed sense of perspective on the entire project.

A final acknowledgment is owed to the Ford Foundation, which has supported not only the collection of the data themselves, but also efforts such as this to disseminate the findings in an accessible way.

Greg J. Duncan
Ann Arbor, Michigan
April, 1983

Contents

Foreword
 —Lee Rainwater   v

Preface
 —Greg J. Duncan   ix

Introduction
 —Greg J. Duncan   1

Chapter 1
An Overview of Family Economic Mobility
 —Greg J. Duncan with James N. Morgan   9

 Methods for Analyzing Change, 11
 Extent of Change in Economic Status, 12
 Accounting for Change in Economic Status, 14
 Effects of the Changing Demographic Structure of the
  Population, 17
 The Role of Family Composition Changes, 18
 The Economic Importance of the Family, 22
 The Unimportance of Attitudes, 24
 Labor Force Participation, 25

The Role of Various Undesirable Events, 26
Summary, 27
Notes, 29

Chapter 2
The Dynamics of Poverty
—Greg J. Duncan with Richard D. Coe and Martha S. Hill   33

Measures of Poverty, 35
Money Income as a Faulty Measure of Resources, 36
The Official Poverty Line as a Faulty Measure of Needs, 36
The Importance of the Accounting Period, 37
Patterns of Annual Poverty, 38
Turnover and Longer-Run Poverty, 40
Raising the Poverty Standard, 42
Changes in the Persistence of Long-Run Poverty, 43
What Can Patterns of Poverty Tell Us about its Nature? 43
Explaining Short- and Long-Run Poverty, 45
Characteristics of the Short- and Longer-Term Poor, 48
Work Hours, Wage Rates, and Poverty, 53
   Effects of Low Work Hours and Unemployment, 53
   Effects of Low Wage Rates, 54
What Causes Some of the Poor to Improve their Status? 55
Summary, 60
Implications, 61
Notes, 65

Chapter 3
The Dynamics of Welfare Use
—Greg J. Duncan with Richard D. Coe   71

Incidence of Welfare Program Participation, 74
Combining Welfare and Work, 78
Patterns of Welfare Use, 78
Characteristics of Welfare Recipients, 79
A Qualitative Look at Welfare Recipients, 81
Intergenerational Aspects of Welfare Use, 82
Effects of Welfare on Family Composition, 83
The "Decision" Not to Participate, 84

Effect of Welfare Income on the Incidence of Poverty, 85
Incidence of Welfare Receipt among Poor Families, 88
Summary and Implications, 89
Notes, 93

Chapter 4
The Dynamics of Work Hours, Unemployment, and Earnings
—Greg J. Duncan with Saul D. Hoffman   **95**

Patterns of Work Hours, 1969–1978, 96
  Average Work Hours, 97
  Patterns of Changes in Work Hours, 98
  Explaining the Patterns, 101
  The Incidence and Cost of Unemployment, 102
Patterns of Earnings, 1969–1978, 106
  Theories of Earnings, 106
    Human capital theory, 106
    Institutional theories, 107
  Determinants of Ten-Year Average Earnings, 109
  Life-Cycle Changes in Earnings, 115
  Patterns of Ten-Year Changes in Earnings, 116
  Patterns of Yearly Change, 119
Summary, 122
Notes, 124

Chapter 5
Recent Trends in the Relative Earnings of Black Men
—Greg J. Duncan with Saul D. Hoffman   **129**

The Nature of Earnings "Poverty" and "Affluence," 132
Explaining the Differences, 135
Theories of Discrimination, 135
Wage Differentials and Discrimination, 137
Effects of Family Background on Schooling and Early Career
  Attainment, 139
Earnings over the Life Cycle, 140
Recent Trends in Relative Earnings, 144
Summary and Implications, 147
Notes, 150

Chapter 6
Do Women "Deserve" to Earn Less than Men?
—Greg J. Duncan with Mary E. Corcoran   **153**

Why Do Women Earn Less than Men? 155
Testing the Skills and Attachment Explanation, 156
     Education, 157
     Work experience, 157
     Work continuity, 160
     Self-imposed restrictions on labor supply, 160
     Absenteeism, 160
Accounting for the Sex-Based Wage Gap, 161
Alternative Explanations, 164
"Old Boy" Networks, 165
Authority, 166
Access to Jobs with Training, 167
Summary and Implications, 167
Notes, 170

References   **173**

Glossary–Index   **181**

Introduction

This book summarizes over ten years of findings from the Panel Study of Income Dynamics. Since 1968, the Survey Research Center of The University of Michigan has been conducting a longitudinal survey on family economic status, collecting data through repeated annual interviews with a single, continuing sample of over 5,000 American families. The picture of changing family and individual economic circumstances that emerges from the longitudinal survey data contradicts many prevailing views about the patterns and causes of economic success or failure, including some inferences commonly drawn from such cross-sectional surveys as the Census Bureau's annual survey of the economic situation of families in the United States. An understanding of these different survey results is important to both social science theory and public policy based on those theories. We hope, with this volume, to make the findings more broadly accessible to those concerned with understanding the nature and extent of poverty and welfare use in this country, with understanding dynamic aspects of work, earnings, and unemployment, and with understanding the economic status of blacks, of women, and of children.

Cross-sectional surveys and longitudinal surveys provide different views of the population being sampled in much the same way that snapshots and motion pictures provide different views of their subjects. Essentially, the Panel Study's focus on reinterviewing a single, representative sample of families over many years provides an extra dimension of information not available even from a long series of cross-sectional surveys. The latter consists of one-time interviews with a different cross section of families each year and produces a series of numerical snapshots showing, for example, how the population pie is divided into slices representing various income levels. Placed side by side, these annual snapshots can reveal changes in the overall distribution of family income—the number of families at each income level. However, they cannot reveal whether individuals or families remain in the same income slice from year to year or move to higher or lower levels. Consequently, inferences about the patterns and causes of family economic change that are frequently drawn from cross-sectional survey data can, quite simply, be wrong.

The Panel Study of Income Dynamics began like a cross-sectional survey, with a representative cross section of families; but in following this sample longitudinally over the years the Panel Study reveals the extent to which individuals and families may move from one economic level to another. Background information furnished about these families' characteristics can be used to provide insight into the possible causes of their subsequent economic successes or misfortunes because it can be linked with the information about changes in their economic status.

Above all, the findings from Panel Study data demonstrate the hazards of using cross-sectional survey data to make inferences about the extent and the causes of change. For example, the Census Bureau's annual "snapshots" show a steady decline in the extent of poverty during the 1960s but little change during the 1970s. The estimated fraction of the population living in families with incomes below the poverty line in 1959 was a little over one-fifth (22 percent), but had dropped to about one-eighth (12 percent) in both 1969 and 1979. (See Chapter 2 for a more complete picture of Census Bureau poverty counts.) Year-to-year changes in these fractions are typically less than 1 percent, and the Census surveys' other measures show little change in the characteristics of the poor from one year to the next: They have shown repeatedly that the individuals who are poor are more likely to be in families headed by a woman, by someone with lower education, and by blacks.

Evidence that one-eighth of the population was poor in two consecutive years, and that those poor shared similar characteristics, is consistent with an inference of absolutely no turnover in the poverty population. Moreover, the evidence seems to fit the stereotype that those families that are poor are likely to remain poor, and that there is a hard-core

population of poor families for whom there is little hope of self-improvement. But the same evidence is equally consistent with a 100 percent
turnover—or any other percentage one might pick—assuming only that
equal numbers of people with similar characteristics cross into and out of
poverty. And in fact, the longitudinal data from the Panel Study reveal
that an astonishing amount of turnover takes place in the low-income
population: *Only a little over one-half of the individuals living in poverty
in one year are found to be poor in the next, and considerably less than
one-half of those who experience poverty remain persistently poor over
many years.*

In the social sciences, most of the empirical studies on families and
individuals have been conducted using data drawn from cross-sectional
surveys. This survey information is used most extensively in labor market and family studies done by economists and demographers, but is also
widely used by sociologists and, to a lesser degree, by psychologists.
Much has been learned from these surveys, especially from those that
are repeated so that several snapshot pictures can be compared. Inge-
nious statistical methods have been applied to cross-sectional information to test theories of the dynamic processes that lead to the circumstances of the population at a point in time.

But Panel Study findings contradict much of what has been inferred
from cross-sectional survey information about the patterns and causes of
change. Consider the question of how much families change their relative economic position over time. The Census Bureau's successive snapshots of how family income is distributed over the entire population
show few changes in the extent of income inequality over the years. The
size of the slice of the income "pie" distributed each year to the richest
families has been fairly constant, as has been the size of the smaller
slices going to the middle income and the poorest families, suggesting
that people's economic positions are permanent and stable. But Panel
Study information on the economic status of the same families and individuals over time shows that this apparent stability is an illusion produced by the offsetting effect of many substantial upward and downward
changes. Fewer than one-half of the population remained in the same
economic position from the late 1960s to the late 1970s, while one-third
had dramatic improvements in their economic well-being and one-fifth
had dramatic declines. And, contrary to popular belief, most of the
population kept their incomes rising faster than inflation, despite the
turbulent economic conditions of that decade.

Consider the related question of why the economic status of some families has come to be so much higher than that of others. Data from cross-sectional surveys show the characteristics of families with high and low economic status—the composition of the income they receive, their patterns of work in the market and at home, the formal training that family members have acquired, and the attitudes and social class background of the family. But a look at families at a point in time ignores the fact that the composition of many families changes radically over time, through children leaving home to form new families, through death, through divorce, and through marriages that unite two families into one. These changes are neither infrequent nor unimportant. Our findings from the Panel Study families we have followed over the years indicate that nearly one-half of the families in any given year will be headed by someone other than the person who headed the "same" family eleven years earlier. Indeed, families change so often and so fundamentally that the very notion of a family is ambiguous in this dynamic context. Furthermore, we find that changes in family composition, rather than the characteristics of family members, account for much of the change in the economic status of the population.

Consider the nature of the welfare system. Administrative records show how much we spend on welfare programs each year and how many families receive income from welfare sources at any given time. Placed side by side, the annual statistics show substantial growth in the welfare rolls over the past several decades, with close to one-tenth of the population now receiving benefits in one form or another. As with poverty, these yearly figures are taken as evidence that the typical welfare case is on the rolls for a long time; some point to these figures as evidence that the welfare system may actually trap generations of families into long-term dependency. For example, in Martin Anderson's (1978) influential book, he states that the welfare system has "created a new caste of Americans—perhaps as much as one-tenth of this nation—a caste of people almost totally dependent on the state, with little hope or prospect of breaking free. Perhaps we should call them the Dependent Americans" (p. 56).

But Panel Study information on the patterns of welfare use during the late 1960s and 1970s shows that while nearly one-quarter of the population received income from welfare sources at least once in the decade, only about 2 percent of all the population could be characterized as dependent upon this income for extended periods of time. Many families receiving welfare benefits at any given time were in the early stages of recovering from an economic crisis caused by the death, departure, or disability of a husband, a recovery that often lifted them out of welfare when they found full-time employment, or remarried, or both. Furthermore, most of the children raised in welfare families did not themselves receive welfare benefits after they left home and formed their own households.

The hazards of making inferences about the dynamics of change from cross-sectional information also apply to attempts to explain what determines the way labor income is distributed differentially among individuals. Is there something about individuals, or their environments, or the larger socioeconomic structure that leads some to earn incomes that are many times larger than those earned by others? At any point in time, there are consistent differences between the successful and unsuccessful in average levels of education, age, socioeconomic background, cognitive ability, occupational position, and demographic characteristics. When data from single cross-sectional surveys are subjected to statistical procedures to compare "otherwise identical" individuals who differ on such measures as level of education, points on an IQ scale, or years of work experience, results showing that additional years of work experience increase earnings faster for the young than for the old are taken as indicative of the life-cycle earnings pattern of a typical worker. Similarly, results showing that minorities and women are consistently overrepresented in certain low-wage occupations and industries are taken as support for the existence of a "dual labor market" economy (a theoretical view that jobs are either "good," with high pay, security, and chances for advancement; or "bad," without these characteristics), one in which women and minorities are locked into the bad jobs. But in varying degrees, these inferences about labor market dynamics are contradicted by the Panel Study's repeated observations on the same individuals. We find that year-to-year fluctuations in the labor market positions of individuals are surprisingly large, and that very few workers receive steady year-to-year increases in earnings. The large amount of job and earnings mobility we have observed for most workers contradicts the view that many of them are locked into certain types of jobs.

Consider the common notion that attitudes play a role in economic success or misfortune. At any point in time, the most successful people also appear to be highly motivated, oriented toward the future, and imbued with a sense of control over life's events. But an association between such positive attitudes and success when both are observed at a single point in time does not prove that the attitudes caused the success. The causation may run the other way, with the success producing the positive attitudes. Or perhaps some third factor, such as the amount of schooling, causes both the greater success and the more positive attitudes. With information on the same individuals and families over time, one can see whether those whose attitudes were initially more positive had greater subsequent success. Panel Study data show that in fact initial attitudes are very weak predictors of either positive or negative subsequent achievement, both among low-income households and among workers in other economic strata.

Successive cross-sectional surveys have shown dramatic improvement in the economic position of black workers over the past two decades. When compared to the average white male worker, the average black male worker earned less than three-fifths as much in the late 1950s, two-thirds as much in the late 1960s, and just over three-quarters as much in the late 1970s. This evidence is usually taken to indicate that black workers are narrowing the economic gap in their status relative to their white counterparts. But comparisons of two years of cross-sectional data on workers in a given age range (e.g., comparing workers aged 25–54 in 1969 with workers aged 25–54 in 1979) are comparing different sets of workers. Some would remain in the specified 25–54 age range at both points in time and would properly be part of the wage comparison. But some older workers from the earlier year would be excluded from the later year when they would be over 54, and would be "replaced" by a new group of younger workers who would have entered the age ranges of 25–54 between the earlier and the later years. Panel Study data show that more than half of the apparent improvement in the wages of black workers between the late 1960s and late 1970s can be attributed to the favorable position of the youngest black workers and not to the gradual improvement in the relative position of blacks who were working during the entire time.

These are just some of the surprising findings to emerge from the Panel Study data. These findings raise some unexpectedly contradictory implications for both current social science theory and for the social and economic policies based on that existing body of theory. While the primary task of this book is to make the study's descriptive findings accessible to a broader audience, we have also attempted to interpret the evidence in light of both current theory (primarily economic) and, when appropriate, current and potential future policy.

The mixture of description, interpretation, and policy discussion varies according to the topic of each chapter, and in general, theories of labor market processes and individual earnings are developed in more depth than are theories of family income and behavior. Chapter 1, covering family well-being, is primarily descriptive; and Chapters 2 and 3, on poverty and welfare use, combine description and interpretation. Chapters 4, 5, and 6, which cover earnings mobility and earnings differences between the races and sexes, rest more heavily on the theories that have been developed to explain labor market phenomena.

Finally, as we go to press in mid-1983, we note that many dramatic economic events have taken place since 1979, including numerous changes in tax and spending policies, major inflation, and the worst recession since World War II. Do these events constitute such fundamental changes in economic conditions that our results from data spanning the 1968–1979 period can provide no lessons for the 1980s?

There are many reasons to suspect that our results are quite applicable to both the present and the future. In the first place, the twelve years prior to 1980 was hardly a period of tranquil economic stability: in 1974 the rate of inflation was above 10 percent, in 1975 the rate of unemployment was above 9 percent, and the economic shocks from oil price changes during the 1970s have yet to be matched during the 1980s. In the second place, the economic events of the late 1960s and 1970s have been built into some of the analyses, enabling us to gauge the effects of macroeconomic conditions on the microeconomic level of individual families. While it is possible to find such macroeconomic effects, they are more often swamped by the huge changes that are constantly occurring at the micro level. For example, during the worst part of the mid-1970s recession, the fraction of families found to be poor in two successive years was several percent higher than average. Nevertheless, among those families found to be poor in 1974, over one-third had *left* poverty in 1975—the worst year of that recession. These and similar findings give us confidence that most of the basic patterns observed during the 1970s will show up in the data that we continue to collect during the 1980s.

1

An Overview of
Family Economic Mobility

To what extent do families actually move from one economic level to another over time? A prevailing view seems to be that, except for periods of unusually extreme economic expansion or recession, the vast majority of American families experience little change, with only slow and incremental movement for some from one economic level to another. This view is not surprising, given that families generally get most of their income from the labor market where nominal wage and salary income seems to increase modestly, but steadily, over time.[1] After adjusting for inflation, the real pay increases are somctimes positive, sometimes negative, but these gains or losses rarely seem to amount to more than a few percentage points. Other sources of family income do fluctuate, but these sources are often intended to offset changes in labor income—for example, unemployment benefits to compensate for lost job income, child support or welfare payments to offset labor income lost when one parent departs, or Social Security benefits and pension payments to cushion labor income lost because of retirement.

No one would argue that most incomes are completely stable. Unemployment benefits can run out, child-support orders may not be paid, and some occupations, especially those of the self-employed or that involve seasonal or otherwise irregular work, may lead to substantial instability. Furthermore, it is easy to point to a number of families who, by their own efforts or by good fortune, have pulled themselves out of poverty, or lifted their economic status from the middle to the upper-middle class, or, through bad fortune or lack of effort, have suffered sharp declines in economic well-being. So while stability would seem to be the norm, some exceptions do arise.

In this chapter we seek to answer our opening question by examining the actual patterns and causes of change in families' economic status using Panel Study data for the eight-year period from 1971 through 1978. We have been following this national sample of families since 1967, and while the economic volatility of the 1971–1978 period differs substantially from the economic tranquillity of the 1967–1971 period, our results for both periods consistently confirm that families actually undergo substantial economic changes over relatively short periods.[2]

When we compare the economic position of the population in two years, 1971 and 1978, we find a remarkable amount of change at all income levels. Of those who were either at the top or at the bottom levels in 1971, only about half had remained in those relative positions in 1978. More surprising, a look at growth in economic status over time shows that a majority managed to keep their incomes growing faster than inflation despite the rapid inflation and severe recession. Next, when we examine our data more closely, we find that neither differences in the personality traits or skills of the family members nor events such as unemployment or disability can account well for these widespread changes. Instead, we find that the single most important factor accounting for changes in family well-being was a fundamental change in family structure: divorce, death, marriage, birth, or a child leaving home. In other words, changes in the economic status of families are linked inextricably to changes in the composition of families themselves. Indeed, the variety and frequency of observed family composition changes are great enough to make the very concept of "family" ambiguous when placed in a dynamic context. Adding to a growing body of evidence about the economic importance of the family, these findings suggest that individuals may have more control over their economic status through decisions about marriage, divorce, procreation, or sharing households with relatives or friends, than they do about seeking more work or better-paying jobs.

Although family composition changes were best able to account for changes in economic status, other events also made a difference. Movements into and out of the labor force mattered, but not as much as did increases or decreases in work hours for those who remained in the labor force continuously. And finally, looking at the incidence and effects of a host of undesirable life events, we find such events to be surprisingly widespread but not as powerful in accounting for changes in well-being as are changes in family composition.

Methods for Analyzing Change

Because the Panel Study has followed a large, representative sample of families over time, it can provide a great deal of information on the extent of short-term family economic mobility.[3] *Total family money income* is the most common yardstick of economic status, and is one of the measures we use.[4] This measure does suffer from various deficiencies: a major drawback is that a given amount of family income may provide very different living standards for families of different sizes and in different situations. However, family size adjustments can be made by using the federal government's annually calculated poverty thresholds for families with different compositions based on the number, sex, and age of family members. In 1978 the poverty line was approximately $2,300 plus $1,000 for each family member.[5] (The $2,300 figure is an estimate of the basic "overhead cost" of maintaining a family.) Thus the approximate poverty threshold in 1978 for a family of two members was $4,300, and for a family of four, it was $6,300. To estimate a family's level of economic well-being in terms of these differing family needs, a second measure, the *income-to-needs* ratio, is obtained by dividing a family's income by its poverty threshold. For example, for a family of four with an income of $12,600 in 1978, income/needs would be a ratio of 2 ($12,600/$6,300), indicating the family's income is twice as high as its poverty threshold. Similarly, for a family of four with an income of $4,200, income/needs would be 2/3—i.e., a ratio less than 1 indicates income lower than poverty level.

Thus armed with our representative sample of families and our two measures of economic well-being—family income and the ratio of family income/needs—it would seem a simple matter to use the family as our unit of analysis for calculating changes in economic status. But a fundamental problem arises from the fact that some of our families have undergone dramatic changes in family composition. For example, in a divorce, one family splits into two, and each then has its own level of family well-being (usually higher for the new family of the husband than the new family of the wife). For the purpose of measuring changes in family well-being, how should we treat the family that is split by divorce during our observation period: Should it be counted as two families, one of which has undergone substantially more of a change in well-being than the other? Or, if it is counted as one family, which "final" family should be chosen? The same situation presents itself in the case of an older child leaving home and setting up his or her own household. The parental family will have smaller needs and possibly smaller income, while the newly formed family of the child will probably be much smaller and have a much smaller income as well. Although it does make sense to compare the status of the newly formed family of the child to the status of the parental family several years earlier, this is not what we usually think of as a change in family well-being.

One solution might be to exclude the radically changed families—perhaps treat them separately—and restrict attention to changes in the economic status of unchanged families. However, that would exclude a very large segment of the population: By the eleventh year of the Panel Study, nearly half of the families were headed by someone other than the person who had headed the "same" family eleven years before. Given such pervasive changes in family composition, it becomes very difficult to define "the family" for use as the unit of analysis in studying the dynamics of change over time.

But while families may change almost beyond recognition, individuals retain their identity and the economic fortunes of each individual can also be identified. Indeed, the family composition changes can be used to help account for the changes in well-being that are observed for the individuals. At any given time, individuals are assembled into family units (including units of a single person), they can be identified by their relationship to the head of that family, and their level of economic well-being can be measured by that family's income or income/needs. Thus, for this chapter, the unit of analysis chosen is the individual.

Extent of Change in Economic Status

A common way of illustrating the changing economic position of a population is by comparing its family income position at two points in time, as is done in Table 1.1 for the representative sample of individuals from the Panel Study for the years 1971 and 1978. In place of actual dollar amounts, we use five levels ("quintiles") of family income to represent a range of family income positions from the first ("highest") to the fifth ("lowest"). These quintiles are formed by a process that arranges all the individuals in a single line according to family income, with individuals in the richest families at one end and those in the poorest families at the other. The line is then divided into quintiles—five segments with equal numbers of individuals in each. For example, if there were 1,000 individuals altogether, each of the five quintiles would in-

Table 1.1

ESTIMATED FRACTIONS OF THE U.S. POPULATION IN VARIOUS COMBINATIONS
OF 1971 AND 1978 FAMILY INCOME QUINTILES

Family Income Quintile in 1971	Family Income Quintile in 1978					
	Lowest	Fourth	Third	Second	Highest	All
Lowest	11.1%	4.4%	1.9%	1.4%	1.2%	20.0%
Fourth	4.3	6.9	4.3	2.7	1.8	20.0
Third	2.7	4.7	6.1	3.7	2.8	20.0
Second	1.2	3.0	5.1	6.3	4.4	20.0
Highest	0.7	0.9	2.8	5.9	9.7	20.0
All	20.0%	19.9%	20.2%	20.0%	19.9%	100.0%

Table reads: "Of all individuals in 1971, 20.0% lived in families whose incomes placed them in the lowest income quintile, but just 11.1% of all individuals placed in the lowest quintile in both 1971 and 1978. The other 8.9% had moved upward to the fourth (4.4%), third (1.9%), second (1.4%), or highest (1.2%) quintiles."

clude 200 individuals; the 200 richest would form the highest income quintile, the next richest 200 would form the second quintile, and so on, down to the lowest quintile, consisting of the poorest 200 individuals.

The use of quintiles implicitly assumes that economic status is based on relative positions, rather than on absolute dollar amounts, and thus while income in dollars may change, an individual's economic position changes only if his or her family income increases or decreases more than an average percentage increase or decrease for everyone else in the same starting position. In 1971, the highest quintile had family incomes of at least $18,500, while the lowest had family incomes below $6,132. By 1978, inflation and real income growth had pushed the highest and lowest quintile breakpoints to about $32,100 and $9,000, respectively.

Table 1.1 provides estimates of the fractions of the nation's population falling into the various combinations of 1971 and 1978 family income quintiles.[6] The first entry, 11.1 percent, indicates that 11.1 percent of the population lived in families with incomes below $6,132 in 1971 *and* below $9,000 in 1978. The "All" column on the right side of the table confirms that, by definition, one-fifth of all individuals lived in families with incomes in the bottom quintile in 1971, so that the fraction of those who ended up at the bottom is only a little over one-half (11.1/20.0) of those who began there. Of course, some of those moving out of the bottom quintile did not go very far, but nearly one-quarter (4.5/20.0) moved into the top three quintiles. These figures suggest a substantial and perhaps surprising degree of income mobility at the bottom end of the income distribution.[7]

Income mobility in the top income quintile was as great as it was at the bottom. Of all individuals living in families with incomes high enough to place them in the top fifth of the income distribution in 1971, more than one-fifth (4.4/20.0) had fallen into the lower three quintiles by 1978, and less than half (9.7/20.0) stayed in the top. Income position can hardly be considered very permanent if the chance of staying on top for those who begin there is only one in two.[8] Note also that "staying on top" is defined here as two times separated by seven years. The fraction who are persistently in the top quintile year after year is even less.

Family income mobility is pervasive at all income levels. In all, nearly one-quarter (23.1 percent) of the sample moved at least two quintile positions in either direction, about three-eighths (36.8 percent) moved at least one, and only two-fifths (40.1 percent) of the population remained in the same relative income position.[9]

Family income position is determined by the number and success of earners in the family plus any transfer or asset income received. The ratio of family income to needs adjusts family income for family size and would be expected to produce mobility patterns different from those of income alone if changes in family size did not accompany, on average, corresponding changes in family income. Some family composition changes may reduce both needs and income (for example, when a child leaves home, needs and income are usually decreased in both the original and the split-off households, though usually more for the child's than for the parents'). Some may increase both needs and income (for example, when two wage-earners marry). Still others may increase one—needs or income—while decreasing the other (for example, when the birth of a child leads to a reduction in a parent's market work but increases family size). The net effect of these changes, however, is to produce a picture of relative income/needs mobility that is remarkably similar to the income mobility depicted in Table 1.1. Similar proportions remained in the same income/needs quintile (39.8 percent), moved one quintile (39.0 percent), moved two or more quintiles (21.2 percent), or moved well out of the bottom or top ends of the income/needs distribution. It is only when patterns of change in economic status for various subgroups of the population are examined that differences appear.

Accounting for Change in Economic Status

Changes in economic status are common, occurring as frequently to families in the bottom and top income quintiles as to those in the middle, and it is important to try to account for these changes. Is there something about some individuals or their environments that causes them to do much better than others? The social sciences have made many attempts to answer this fundamental question but theories about the roles of attitudes, skills, institutions, and demographic characteristics are difficult to test. Fortunately, the Panel Study provides data that allow a host of factors to be roughly ordered in terms of their ability to account for the variety of changes in economic status that families experience. Although we cannot obtain a complete understanding of, say, all of the ways in which an involuntary job loss affects a family's status, we can show whether involuntary job losses are sufficiently frequent and dramatic in their effects to explain more about patterns of change in family economic fortunes than can such other factors as moving to the Sun Belt, having a child, joining a union, or being more motivated.

Our analysis will distinguish between two types of explanatory variables—"initial characteristics" and "events."[10] Each family entered the study period with a set of initial characteristics, and we have measures of a number of potentially important attitudes, behavior patterns, skills, and demographic characteristics of each household head.[11] The specific measures are listed in the box. There are reasons to suspect that each of these characteristics may play a role in distinguishing those with subsequent economic success and failure.

MEASURES OF THE INITIAL CHARACTERISTICS OF THE HOUSEHOLD HEAD

Attitudes
  Achievement motivation
  Sense of personal efficacy
  Orientation toward the future

Behavior Patterns
  Avoidance of undue risk
  Connections to sources of information and help

Skills
  Years of completed education
  A "test score" measure of cognitive ability

Demographic Characteristics
  Race
  Age

But we also suspect that events may play a role in explaining why some families do better than others. Among such events we include family composition changes, movements into and out of the labor force, births, the departure of children from their parental home, long-distance residential moves, disablement, job loss and unemployment, and changes in union status. These events also play the role of "intervening" variables and may help to explain why the initial characteristics have the effects that they do. If, for example, the more highly educated individuals do better, then it is important to know which favorable events occurred more frequently for them or which unfavorable events occurred less frequently. In other words, the events may help answer the question of how education operated to produce the favorable changes in economic status.

As a measure of change in economic status, we computed an average annual growth rate in family income and income/needs and, where appropriate, in the hourly and annual earnings of the household head. The time interval, again, was 1971 to 1978, but the growth rate measures were calculated from all of the annual observations from 1971 to 1978, not just from the beginning and ending years. In addition, the Consumer Price Index was used to inflate each dollar figure to 1978 price levels, so the calculated growth rate is real rather than nominal. Families with positive real growth rates are those who did better than inflation, and families with negative growth rates are those who did worse. The size of the growth rate figure is analogous to a compound interest rate. For example, over a seven-year period, an annual real growth rate of 10 percent will double a family's real income or income/needs just as a 10 percent interest rate will double the amount in one's savings account in seven years.[12] Similarly, in seven years, a positive 5 percent annual growth rate will increase a $20,000 income to $28,000; a negative 5 percent rate will decrease a $20,000 income to $14,000.

Table 1.2 shows the average growth rates and their dispersion for income and income/needs for the population as a whole. Several startling facts emerge. First, despite the turbulent economic conditions of the seventies, with high inflation rates and a severe recession, slightly more than half the population lived in families in which incomes kept up with inflation, and nearly three-fifths kept up in terms of the more comprehensive measure of economic status—income/needs. Furthermore, consistent with the picture of change shown earlier, half the population lived in households where family incomes and family income/needs either increased or decreased dramatically (at more than a five

Table 1.2

GROWTH IN REAL INCOME AND INCOME/NEEDS, 1971–1978
(All Sample Individuals)

	Income	Income/Needs
Kept up with inflation	54%	59%
Annual real growth rate exceeded 5 percent	27	32
Annual real growth rate was between −5%and +5%	49	49
Annual real growth rate was less than −5%	24	19
Total	100%	100%

Table reads: "More than half (54 percent) of all individuals lived in families in which family income grew at least as fast as the rate of inflation between 1971 and 1978."

percent real annual growth rate). With both measures of economic status, relatively modest growth rates were the exception rather than the rule.

That most of the population more than kept up with inflation seems surprising, but there are several reasons why this is the case. First, many people apparently misperceive their success in keeping incomes rising with inflation. As Juster (1979) has pointed out, inflation is a continual process, visible each week at the grocery store or at the gasoline pump, while income increases occur very infrequently, often just once a year. Second, aggregate statistics indicate that per capita personal income almost kept pace with inflation; its real growth between 1971 and 1978 was negative but very small, −.15 percent. Whether most families keep up with inflation will depend upon the *distribution* of individual family growth rates around the average. It is quite possible to have no real growth, *on average*, when a small proportion of families experience large income losses (as around retirement) and a large proportion of families experience modest but positive real income growth. Also, new families with low incomes are constantly forming over time, while older families with higher incomes are leaving the population. In short, moderate income increases can be quite widespread even when aggregate (average) income per capita stays constant.

Effects of the Changing Demographic Structure of the Population

The fact that income/needs kept up with inflation better than income alone suggests that, on average, family composition changes were more commonly of the sort that tended either to reduce needs more than income or to increase income more than needs. And indeed this was the case. The decade of the seventies saw unusually low birth rates while at the same time the baby boom children began moving out of their parental homes in record numbers. Births add to the family needs standard and (if the mother drops out of the labor force) decrease family income. But when adult children leave home, the economic well-being of family members left behind is usually increased, since the departing children typically consumed more family income than they earned. Thus the offsetting effect of few births and many departures has tended to increase the income/needs position of a substantial portion of the population, resulting in more success in keeping income/needs growth ahead of inflation than in keeping income growth alone ahead of inflation. These trends will not persist indefinitely, since the baby boom children will all leave home eventually and birth rates may change.

The Role of Family Composition Changes

Since the early years of the Panel Study, there have been repeated attempts to gauge the relative importance of a variety of attitudes, skills, and events in accounting for changes in family economic status. All, including this examination of the 1971 to 1978 period, have indicated that changes in the composition of families are sufficiently frequent and dramatic in their effects to rank first in importance. However, two qualifications must be noted.

First, the economic status of men was affected far less by family composition changes than was that of women. This results from several facts: on average, women earn much less than men; after a divorce or separation, children typically live with the mother rather than the father; and compensatory private income transfers such as payments of alimony and child support are likely to be infrequent and insufficient to make up very much of the lost income.[13]

Second, the relative importance of family composition changes does not imply that other events or characteristics were totally unimportant. Quite the contrary, a number of these other factors had substantial (and certainly statistically significant) effects on family well-being. But the extent to which an event can account for the diverse patterns of change in family well-being depends upon the size of the effect and the frequency with which the event occurs. On this score, family composition change was clearly the most important event.

The effects of family composition changes on changes in economic status during the 1971 to 1978 period are shown in Table 1.3 for the three groups that are most affected by them: adult women who began the 1971 to 1978 period as unmarried heads of their own households, adult women who were married, and young children (age 1 to 14 years old).[14] The table shows the changes in real family income levels (i.e., 1978 family income minus 1971 family income) as well as the average annual growth rates in real income and income/needs associated with various family composition changes that these individuals experienced. The latter two measures were adjusted statistically for the effects of a set of demographic measures.[15]

The first group shown on Table 1.3 are the women who began the period as unmarried heads of their own households. While most (80.8 percent) remained unmarried, more than one-sixth had married by the end of the period. (A very small number had undergone more complicated changes such as marriage followed by divorce.) The difference in the financial fortunes of these two groups is striking. Those who married enjoyed inflation-adjusted family income increases that were about $14,500 more ($15,357 − $864) than those who remained unmarried. Adjusted annual growth rates in family income were also much higher (+10 percent versus −1 percent).[16] Since marriage may increase not only income but also family size and hence family needs, the growth in income/needs associated with marriage was not quite as dramatic as the growth of income alone.

The economic status of the women who began the period married is equally dependent upon family composition changes, particularly divorce. As the data in Table 1.3 show, the women who remained married enjoyed improvements in economic status while those who divorced suffered declines; the differences between them amounted to more than $10,000 in their incomes, more than 10 percent in their income growth rates, and more than 6 percent in their income/needs growth rates. As mentioned before, many factors contribute to the devastating economic effects of divorce upon women: Women cannot command earnings levels as high as those of men; children usually remain with their mothers after divorce, increasing the needs of the mother's new family while reducing her likelihood of having a full-time job; and alimony and child support payments are inadequate to maintain a divorced woman at the standard of living she had when married. Hoffman (1977a) found that fewer than half of the divorced or separated women received any alimony or child support payments from the absent husbands and fathers, and that for

Table 1.3

EFFECTS OF FAMILY COMPOSITION CHANGES ON CHANGES IN ECONOMIC STATUS
FOR WOMEN AND CHILDREN, 1971–1978

Group and Change	Percent of Group	Family Income		Family Income/Needs
		1978 minus 1971	Adjusted Average Annual Growth Rate	Adjusted Average Annual Growth Rate
Female Heads in 1972:				
Remained unmarried	80.8%	$ 864	–.9%	0.4%
Married	18.6	15,357	10.0	7.0
Wives in 1972:				
Remained married	84.8	3,086	0.7	1.2
Widowed	7.7	–5,267	–5.4	–0.8
Divorced or separated	7.8	–7,385	–9.4	–5.3
Children aged 1–14 in 1972:				
Parents stayed married	68.1	6,995	3.3	2.7
Child left home	9.0	–9,002	–9.2	–1.1
Parents divorced	5.3	–6,602	–8.7	–5.8
Female head remained unmarried	7.4	1,088	–0.1	–0.1
Female head married	2.0	10,521	9.4	6.9

Note: All income figures have been inflated to 1978 levels using the Consumer Price Index. Income and income/needs growth rates have been adjusted for differences in age, education, and race. These adjustments account for why some family income changes are positive and yet corresponding growth rates are negative.

Table reads: "Of the group of unmarried women who were heads of their own households in 1972, 80.8% remained unmarried. For those remaining unmarried, real (inflation-adjusted) family income rose by an average of $864. . . ."

those who did receive such payments, the amounts averaged less than $2,600 per year for white women and $1,500 per year for black women.[17]

Women who became widowed also did worse, although the economic effects were not as strong as with divorce. Income fell substantially, but so did needs, so the income/needs growth rate for women who became widowed was only slightly negative.

Young children (ages 1 to 14 in 1972 and 7 to 20 in 1978) obviously had little or no control over decisions or events that affected their family economic well-being. Changes in their economic status were dramatically tied to changes in family composition—in fact, for these children, family composition changes explained more of their changes in economic status than for any other group.

By the end of the period, children living in families that changed as a result of a divorce or separation had experienced severe drops in economic well-being. Even after adding in any amounts received as alimony, child support, or welfare payments, their family incomes fell $6,600, or over 8 percent annually, and their income/needs fell by more than half that amount. Although these children constituted only about one-twentieth of the entire group of children, they carried a disproportionately large burden of economic misfortune, mirroring and magnifying the previously mentioned devastating economic effects of divorce or separation on the mothers with whom they usually lived. The situations of these children are striking evidence of the far reaching, unsolved economic problems posed by family disruption.

By contrast, children living in families in which an initially unmarried mother became married did very well, a contrast which also held in comparing them with children living with an initially unmarried mother who remained unmarried throughout the period. Of the remaining children, most were in unchanged two-parent families, and did quite well: real income grew by about $7,000 from 1971 through 1978, and their adjusted growth in income was about 3.3 percent per year.

Finally, the effects on children of a somewhat different kind of family composition change—the formation of new, second-generation households—is represented by those older children who, by 1978, had left home. Although these children had substantially lower family incomes in their split-off households than in their parental households, their income/needs ratios, on average, were reduced only modestly.

The relation between family composition changes and economic fortunes is summarized in Table 1.4, which presents estimates of the fractions of the interpersonal variation in income and income/needs growth

Table 1.4
FRACTION OF VARIATION IN GROWTH OF INCOME AND INCOME/NEEDS,
1971–1978, EXPLAINED BY FAMILY COMPOSITION CHANGE
(Various Groups of Sample Individuals)

Group Experiencing Change	Fraction of Income Variation Explained	Fraction of Income/Needs Variation Explained
Male household heads in 1972	2.1%	0.2%
Wives in 1972	11.5	4.7
Female household heads in 1972	11.9	6.6
Children aged 15–29 in 1972	18.6	7.6
Children aged 1–14 in 1972	23.6	8.9

Table reads: "For the group of adult men who headed their own households in 1972, family composition changes explained 2.1% of the total variation in family income growth rates. . . ."

rates that are accounted for by changes in family composition for all five major demographic groups. The economic fortunes of the four groups of women and children are strikingly dependent upon family composition changes, especially in comparison to the fifth group, adult men, for whom they explain only two percent of the variation in income growth rates and virtually none of the variation in income/needs growth.[18] The findings are all the more striking because it is rare when variables account for more than one or two percentage points of the variation in a measure like income growth. Indeed, for young children, nearly one-quarter of the variation in family income growth could be explained by family composition changes; for family income/needs, the figure is about ten percent. This explanatory power far exceeds that of other events or of initial skills and attitudes.

The Economic Importance of the Family

These findings that changes in family composition account for much of the change in family economic status join an impressive body of evidence on the economic importance of the family. Such evidence has indicated, for example, that the unpaid work done in the home by family members constitutes a substantial share of the nation's economic activity. Additional studies have shown that the resources transferred *within* families are many times more important than governmental or private philanthropic transfers outside it.

It has long been recognized that the economic value of work done at home is not captured by such conventional measures of aggregate economic activity as the Gross National Product, due to measurement problems. Work performed in the labor market is rewarded with a measurable dollar payment.[19] Work performed in the home, unless by a paid housekeeper, is not rewarded by a measurable cash payment, nor is it a simple matter to assign it a dollar value. When Gronau (1980, p.408) used Panel Study data to estimate the dollar value of work done at home by married women his findings indicated that if such work were compensated in dollars it would increase the family's money income by more than 60 percent. Not surprisingly, the estimated value of child care increases with the number of children in the family. The value of housework is so great that when the wife joins the labor force, the loss of her home production is almost equal to her increased money earnings.

The family has also been found (Baerwaldt and Morgan, 1973; and Morgan, 1978) to be society's major means of redistributing income from the smaller numbers of those who earn it in the labor market to the much larger numbers of those who depend on it. *Between* families, these transfers comprise three broad forms: Payment of taxes on personal income, a portion of which subsequently provides assistance to families in need through a variety of governmental transfer programs; private donations to various philanthropic organizations such as United Way; and private transfers of money directly between related family members living in separate households, such as supporting an elderly parent or making child support payments. Not surprisingly, the first of these forms—payment of personal taxes that support governmental transfer programs—accounts for a much larger proportion of these interfamily transfers than do either of the two private forms.

However, transfers *within* families are many times more important than governmental transfers. Morgan (1978) calculated the value of those transfers with Panel Study data by comparing the labor market earnings, dollar value of housework, and amounts from other income sources of family members to an estimate of the share of the family's resources that each family member consumes. Children, of course, are the most prominent group of recipients, while adult men, especially those between the ages of 35 and 54, are the most prominent group of donors. Women who head their own households are net donors as well, as are younger married women when the value of their housework is included. The estimated value of transfers within families in 1975 was over $500 billion, an amount several times as large as governmental transfers in that year and nearly one-third the size of the Gross National Product. In short, despite the growth of government transfer programs, the *family* is still the most important mechanism for income maintenance.

The Unimportance of Attitudes

The idea that "good" or "bad" attitudes explain economic success or failure seems to have widespread appeal. Successful people are typically described (and usually self-described) as motivated, self-confident, ambitious, or driven; the implication is that these personality traits were instrumental in their success. Social psychologists have tried to define, measure, and test such traits for their effects, but much of the evidence about the role of attitudes in determining economic success comes from cross-sectional data gathered at a single point in time. Typically, such data show that successful people have more positive attitudes—a result that agrees with our everyday observations. But did the attitudes cause the success, or did the success cause the attitudes? Or did something else, say educational attainment, cause both the positive attitude and the economic success? It is virtually impossible to infer these patterns of causality from cross-sectional data.

Longitudinal data are much better suited to test for causality, although they still do not give definitive results. Through repeated observations on the same individuals over time, the attitudes observed initially can be studied to determine whether they are related to *subsequent* economic success or failure. Do the initially poor with higher motivation have a better chance of climbing out of poverty? More generally, does economic status improve more for those who began with higher scores on the attitudinal measures?[20] These are propositions that can be put to the test with longitudinal data.

Several attitudinal measures were included in the early Panel Study questionnaires. Here we report on the relative importance of three of them: achievement motivation, sense of personal efficacy (e.g., control over one's life), and orientation toward the future. Our tests (reported in Duncan and Morgan, 1981*b*) consisted of relating the attitudes measured in 1972 to the growth in economic status that occurred between 1971 and 1978. Separate tests were performed for two groups: working men who headed households in 1972 and women (regardless of work status) who headed their own households in 1972. The changes in economic status for both groups were measured in terms of family income and family income/needs, and for the men, changes in hourly earnings and annual labor market earnings were also measured.

In how many instances did those who began with more positive attitudes do better? For personal efficacy and for orientation toward the future, not one out of 32 possible estimated effects was statistically significant at conventional levels. For achievement motivation, there was a positive and significant effect for just one of the sixteen changes in economic status (whether female household heads kept family incomes rising faster than inflation). Given so many separate tests, this single positive result could reflect something found only in the Panel Study sample and not in the population as a whole.

The mass of negative evidence extends far beyond these tests. We have repeatedly performed such tests over different time periods, with different concepts of change in economic status (including climbing out of poverty) and for many different subgroups in the population. We find almost no evidence that initial attitudes affect subsequent economic success.[21]

Labor Force Participation

Although family composition changes provide the best explanation of the changing economic fortunes of individuals, other events also matter. Movement into and out of the labor force, although relatively infrequent especially for men, often has substantial effects on family income. These effects are particularly large if the individual making the change is a man beginning or ending a full-time job. Because women's hourly pay rates and work hours are so much lower than those of men, women's movement into and out of the labor force produces an average change in annual income of only about $2,000; for men, the change is between $7,000 and $9,000. Although these changes may appear substantial, they are neither very common nor are they much larger than those experienced by individuals who work continuously. Of all initially employed male household heads (in 1971), only about 17 percent were not working seven years later. Comparable fractions for initially employed women were considerably higher: 34 percent of the unmarried female household heads and 39 percent of the married women were not working seven years later.

Although substantial income changes from movements into and out of the labor force are inevitable as labor income rises from or falls to zero, surprisingly large changes in labor income often occur for those continuously in the labor force. As detailed in Chapter 4, large variations in work hours are brought about by second jobs, overtime, job changes, and brief spells of unemployment, making changes in labor incomes for employed men the most volatile component of family income.

The Role of Various Undesirable Events

Among the many life events that can be constructed from the Panel Study data, it is important to distinguish those that are particularly adverse. We have cited the unfavorable economic effects of divorce and widowhood. Other adverse events include major unemployment (lasting more than one month), involuntary job loss, major work loss due to illness (lasting more than one month), disability,[22] involuntary residential moves (e.g., evictions), and a major decrease in family income (dropping by half or more).[23] Here we show the prevalence of these involuntary events, and examine their demographic correlates.

Table 1.5 shows the proportion of initially married men who were affected by one or more of these involuntary events during the 11-year period from 1968 to 1978. The final row of the table gives the results for the entire group of men; the first three rows distinguish three different age subgroups. (Note that these age groups are not contiguous.) Involuntary events are surprisingly widespread, with only about one-quarter of these men escaping them altogether and well over half experiencing at least two. Approximately equal numbers of young and old men escaped these events, although the incidence of multiple involuntary events tended to fall disproportionately among those under 60 years of age.

A look at the specific events shows many of the expected age patterns: disability and widowhood increased dramatically with age, while divorce was much more frequent among the young. Two of the work-related events—unemployment and involuntary job loss—were also concentrated among the young.

Given the surprising frequency with which these events occur, it becomes important to ask whether certain characteristics insulate individuals from these disruptive events. Are upper-income families more immune to them? Are the more educated or efficacious less susceptible? To investigate this in a rough, descriptive way, the number of involuntary events experienced by each of the married men was related to the following set of characteristics (measured in 1968): education, age, family income, savings, race, region, city size, and two attitudes—efficacy and future orientation. The results showed that the single most important characteristic was educational attainment. After differences in current

Table 1.5

FREQUENCY OF UNDESIRABLE LIFE EVENTS, BY AGE, 1968–1978
(Married Men in 1968)

Events, 1968–1978	Age Groups in 1968			
	Under 30	40–49	60–69	All Age Groups
At Least 1 Occurrence of:				
Becoming widowed	0%	4%	15%	5%
Becoming divorced	18	6	4	9
Major unemployment	37	24	9	29
Involuntary job changes	33	23	4	22
Work loss due to illness	22	38	14	28
Becoming disabled	17	27	53	30
Involuntary residential moves	25	8	7	13
Major decrease in family income	15	13	23	16
Total number of undesirable events:				
0	27%	19%	25%	27%
1–3	44	44	64	48
4 or more	29	27	11	25

Table reads: "None of the married men under age 30 in 1968 became widowed during the 11-year period of 1968 through 1978."

income, savings, and all other variables were controlled, those with college degrees experienced one less undesirable event, on average, than those with an eighth-grade education. Furthermore, the education effect was nearly as strong among the older men as it was among younger men. What can account for this benefit from educational attainment? It is not because education leads to greater financial success; the effects of education showed up even among men with the same income and savings levels. Nor is it because the highly educated are more efficacious or oriented toward the future because differences in these measures are controlled as well. Furthermore, it does not appear that education has only a short-term credential effect. Its benefits were almost as strong among older men as among younger ones. Apparently something about the skills acquired in school or possibly about the other characteristics of those who completed more schooling (e.g., perseverance or IQ) makes better-educated people more successful at avoiding undesirable life events. We tend to favor the skills explanation, since the beneficial effects of education tend to persist even after IQ and other personality differences have been taken into account.[24]

None of the other variables was as consistently important as education in deterring undesirable life events. Families that began the study with some savings tended to be more successful in this regard, although a high initial income level did not seem to help much. Interestingly, blacks were no more likely to experience the detrimental events than whites once other demographic differences such as education, income, and savings were taken into account.

It is difficult to generalize about the economic consequences of events other than changes in family composition and labor force status. These consequences often differed for young and old, for blacks and whites, and for other demographic divisions of the population, as well as for the time period over which the events and outcomes were measured. Some of the labor market events, in particular unemployment, will be discussed in detail in other chapters. But while many of these other events do have a dramatic impact on some families, none of them appears to account for as much of the fluctuating fortunes of the nation's families as changes in family composition.

Summary

Our evidence indicates that economic well-being fluctuates markedly for individuals over time, with many shifting upward from the lower end of the family income distribution and others shifting downward from the top. By far the most important cause of change is change in family composition—births, deaths, children leaving home, and especially divorce and marriage. The economic status of young children and adult women is particularly sensitive to the effects of divorce and remarriage. The prevalence of family composition changes makes the very definition of a "family" ambiguous over time, and the economic effects of such changes add to growing evidence that the family unit has important economic significance.

Aside from family composition changes, movements into and out of the labor force, especially by men, produce substantial changes in family well-being. However, strikingly large changes in work hours and earnings were also found for those who worked continuously. Very few within the adult labor force actually hold stable, full-time jobs of fifty 40-hour weeks per year.

Although more positive attitudes are found for those at the top end of the income distribution at a point in time, we found little support for the proposition that those with more positive attitudes have more favorable subsequent changes in economic status.

The general picture of family economic mobility, then, is one of substantial yet undirected change, often caused by involuntary events. On the whole, however, more than half of the population lived in families that kept incomes rising faster than inflation during most of the 1970s. This effect was even more pervasive when family incomes were adjusted for family size, because a combination of low birth rates and the departure of large numbers of adult children from parental households produced increased economic well-being for many families.

In the following chapters we turn from an overview of the dynamics of change for families at all levels of economic well-being to examine segments of the population and components of economic status that warrant special interest. The next two chapters focus on the dynamics affecting the lower end of the income distribution—on the poverty population (Chapter 2) and on the welfare population (Chapter 3). The last three chapters examine the way labor market dynamics affect three segments of the work force: Chapter 4 examines the largest segment, white men; Chapter 5 examines black men; and Chapter 6 examines women.

Notes

[1]Throughout this book, inflation-adjusted amounts are termed *real*, while unadjusted amounts are termed *nominal*.

[2]The 1971 to 1978 results are based on Duncan and Morgan (1981a). Earlier work includes Morgan (1974) and Lane and Morgan (1975). Given the large macroeconomic volatility since 1978, it is likely that the extent of change in family status has continued to be at least as large as in these two earlier periods.

[3]For the Panel Study, a "family" consists of related people living together as a family as well as some unrelated people who share nontemporary, family-like living arrangements. See the Glossary for a more detailed definition.

[4]*Total family money income* consists of the following: labor market earnings of all family members; dividend, rent and interest income from financial assets; public income transfers from such sources as Social Security, welfare, and unemployment compensation; and private income transfers such as child support payments.

[5]The poverty line calculations are detailed in Chapter 2. Inflation has already rendered these dollar figures obsolete. The 1978 figures are illustrated here because that is the final year used in the empirical analysis of this chapter.

[6]For readers accustomed to the Census Bureau's distinction between families and unrelated individuals, it should be noted that these two groups are not distinguished in this book; all are considered families even though a family may consist of only one individual. See the Glossary for other details.

[7]Patterns of change for individuals living in or near poverty are detailed in Chapter 2.

[8]As shown below, income losses are much more common for some kinds of individuals (especially older children about to leave home) than others. But even among the most

stable group—the initially married men—the comparable chance of staying on top is less than two in three.·

[9]Any error in reporting or recording income information will produce a spurious appearance of mobility. Panel Study procedures call for repeated interviews with the same respondents, often involving the same interviewer as well. This probably reduces such errors, as does our use of broad quintile ranges rather than exact dollar amounts. However, some of the movement between adjacent quintiles may be the result of errors of this kind.

[10]The details of this analysis are given in Duncan and Morgan (1981).

[11]At the time the Panel Study began, in 1968, accepted practices (notably those followed by the U.S. Bureau of the Census) dictated that in a husband–wife family, the husband was automatically defined as the "household head." A critical review of these practices during the 1970s resulted in adopting new definitions for the 1980 U.S. Census. However, because the Panel Study is a single, continuing study, consistency over time requires using the definitions originally imposed in 1968.

[12]The "Rule of 72" is a way to calculate the growth rates and lengths of time needed to double an amount: the number of years (n) needed to double an amount of money at any growth rate (r) is found by the formula $r \times n = 72$. Thus, if n is seven years, the growth rate needed to double an amount is 72/7, or about 10 percent.

[13]In addition, when alimony and child support payments are made, they ought to be subtracted from the income of the person making those payments. That is not done in the figures presented in this chapter. Hoffman and Holmes (1977) show that it doesn't make much of a difference in the basic findings.

[14]These three groups combined constitute over three-fifths of the entire population.

[15]Age, education, and race were the demographic measures on which statistical adjustments were made. An example of the usefulness of such adjustments may be seen in assessing the impact of becoming widowed. We know that family income grows much less rapidly (if at all) for elderly couples than for young couples just starting out, and becoming widowed occurs much more frequently among older persons. Consequently the income growth rate for women who became widowed would reflect this *age* effect along with any effect of becoming widowed. To estimate the "pure" effect of being widowed, we used a statistical technique (multiple regression) that adjusts for these age-related differentials.

[16]Recall that a 10 percent annual growth rate nearly doubles an amount of income in seven years.

[17]For a comprehensive review of the evidence on the economic consequence of divorce, see Espenshade (1979).

[18]Suppose all of these men either remained married or became divorced. If the income growth rate for every one of those remaining married was, say, 5 percent per year and the income growth rate for every one of those who divorced was, say, 3 percent per year, then the family composition change variable would account for 100 percent of the variation in growth rates. If the *average* growth rates were 5 and 3 percent, respectively, but some individuals in each group were higher or lower than these averages, then family composition changes would account for some but not all of the variation in growth rates. And finally, if the average growth rates for these two groups were identical, then family composition change would account for none of the variation. In data based on a sample of more than 5,000 families, a variable accounting for as little as 1 percent of the variance is statistically significant at conventional levels. The figures shown in Table 1.4 have been adjusted by regression for the effects of age, education, and race.

[19]Some paid market work is performed in the "underground economy," and is difficult to measure in practice.

[20]Even if the evidence suggests a positive response to this question, the issue is not entirely settled, since Panel Study data cannot reveal attitudes or events dating before the first observation. Suppose that just prior to our first observation in 1968 an individual had started a promising entry-level job, giving him reason to feel optimistic and even enthusiastic about the future. Our initial measurement of his attitudes would show a high level, and thus a subsequent finding of economic success would show a correlation of high initial attitudes with subsequent success. However, the job might not only be responsible for the subsequent success but also for the positive attitudes found on our first observation.

[21]One troubling possible explanation for negative evidence of this kind is that the attitudes are so poorly measured that they do not distinguish between those with truly different attitudes. While measurement error may be present, the fact that there is a substantially positive association between attitudes and the *level* of economic status suggests that error does not dominate the results on change. It is also important to note that our findings on the lack of effects of personal efficacy are contradicted by the work of several authors who have used the National Longitudinal Study data. The controversy is summarized by Andrisani (1977, 1981), Duncan and Morgan (1981), and Duncan and Liker (1983).

[22]Disability is defined by an affirmative response to the question, "Do you have a physical or nervous condition that limits the type of work or the amount of work you can do?" Thus it does not necessarily mean that the respondent is unable to work altogether.

[23]The focus of that analysis (detailed in Duncan and Morgan, 1980) was not on family economic status as an outcome; hence a decrease in family income was considered as one of the events.

[24]See Juster (1976) for a diverse yet thorough analysis of the effects of education on a wide variety of economic outcomes.

2

The Dynamics of Poverty

You have the poor among you always.
    —Matthew 26:11, *New English Bible*

We speak easily of "the poor" as if they were an ever-present and unchanging group. Indeed, the way we conceptualize the "poverty problem" seems to presume the permanent existence of a well-defined group of "poor people" within American society.

A number of different views have been advanced about the causes of poverty and the appropriate solutions. One view holds that poverty is a result of people having inadequate job skills and few opportunities to use the skills they do possess, and that the solution lies in increasing job skills through training programs, or in increasing job opportunities through a vigorous, expanding economy. Another holds that poverty results from certain attitudes, or an entire set of values and beliefs held by poor people—that there is a "culture of poverty." There is little consensus on what might cause such attitudes; they have even been attributed to the very government programs that have been designed to alleviate poverty in the first place. Among the proponents of both views are those who think that the causes of "the poverty problem" are so numerous and poorly understood that the most important issue at the policy level is to address the effects of poverty, with particular concern for children living in poverty. In this approach the most efficient solution is to augment the incomes of the poor with a simple income transfer program. But whatever the view, the stereotype that "the poor" this year will also be "the poor" next year and beyond is seldom questioned. Poverty is seen by most people as a persistent condition of life for its victims.

In order to explore the dynamics of poverty, we must first consider how poverty is defined. Here again, as with opinions about its causes and cures, there are conflicting points of view. One set of critics argues that the official definition of poverty understates its true extent because it is too parsimonious or because it should be geared to changes in the general living standards of society. Another set of critics argues that the official definition overstates the extent of poverty since the benefits of in-kind programs such as food stamps are omitted from the measure of resources.

Both views call for adjustments to estimates of annual income or needs. However, for the purpose of understanding the extent and nature of poverty, neither adjustment is as telling as changing the time period over which income and needs are measured. Examinations of poverty based on data covering one-year periods do not capture the actual volatility of family economic fortunes. This volatility demands that we distinguish between the temporarily and the persistently poor. Because so many policies are designed with a definition of poverty based on annual income and needs, it is crucial to know the extent to which annual figures misclassify the short- and the longer-term poor.

Data from the Panel Study indicate that nearly one-quarter of the U.S. population experienced at least occasional periods of poverty during the course of the decade between 1969 and 1978. However, the number with *persistently* low resources was much lower than one-quarter, and substantially lower than the poverty counts based on single-year Census Bureau information. Individuals with persistently low incomes are not, as some would have it, predominately an "underclass" of young adults living in large urban areas. Rather, persistent poverty falls disproportionately on blacks, on the elderly, and on those living in rural areas and in the South. The persistently poor are more sharply defined by these demographic characteristics than are those found to be poor in a given year. This fact has important implications for programs that seek to aim anti-poverty funds most effectively at geographic areas with only single-year information to define their target. The picture of need in U.S. society, then, is largely one of many people in temporary need, of whom some have the resources to see themselves through difficult times, while others may need temporary assistance. A smaller but by no means insignificant number lives in households in which poverty is the rule rather than the exception.

A related and crucially important question is whether information on the economic well-being of families over many years allows us a better understanding of the causes and nature of longer-term poverty. One-third of those persistently poor are elderly, with little opportunity for improving their own economic positions. But among those who are poor in a given year, we find that many of the nonelderly do improve their economic status and that family composition changes have the most dramatic effect on the poverty status of the individuals living in families headed by women. Indeed, spells of poverty often begin with a divorce but end with remarriage. Finally, we find little evidence that "better attitudes" enable many people to climb out of poverty.

Measures of Poverty[1]

Following President Johnson's declaration of a "war on poverty" in the 1960s, an official poverty measure was needed to help channel aid to the neediest individuals and to help monitor the efficiency of the aid programs. In 1968, the federal government adopted as its operational definition of poverty a set of annual dollar need levels developed by the Social Security Administration, under the direction of Mollie Orshansky. These guidelines, in spite of much discussion and criticism, have re mained firmly entrenched as the main indicators of the country's success in fighting poverty.

The function of a poverty measure is to identify individuals who do not command sufficient economic resources to attain a satisfactory standard of living.[2] The official definition of poverty rests on a comparison of a family's cash income with an estimate of its needs. Family needs, in turn, are based on the number of family members, their ages, and their sex. The heart of the needs standard is an estimate of weekly food costs for individuals of each age and sex, produced by the United States Department of Agriculture.[3] The resulting poverty line in 1978 was roughly $3,300 for an individual living alone, $4,300 for a married couple, and $6,600 for a family of four. If a given family's money income fell short of this poverty line, then the family was deemed "poor"; if it equaled or exceeded this line, it was "nonpoor."

Although few would dispute the concept that poverty involves insufficient resources to meet basic needs, many critics have argued that family cash income is a faulty measure of resources, while others have argued that the official poverty needs standard is a faulty measure of minimal needs in our society. Few of these critics have actively questioned the notion that a single year is a reasonable period of time over which to measure resources and needs. However, these two major lines of argument, reviewed below, raise important questions about the way these measures affect the count and characteristics of the poor.

Money Income as a Faulty Measure of Resources

, Money income is an incomplete measure of a family's potential ability to fulfill basic needs. It omits all of the goods and services such as housework and child care that a household provides rather than purchases for itself as well as the goods and services that a household may receive from others in exchange for its services (without the intermediary use of money). Furthermore, it fails to distinguish the "time poor"—e.g., those whose labor market and housework hours leave virtually no leisure time—from others.[4]

By far the most publicized criticism of money income as a measure of family resources is that it neglects any in-kind benefits—i.e., the benefits families receive from the government in the form of goods or services rather than cash. The largest of these programs are Food Stamps, Medicare, Medicaid, various housing subsidy programs, and aid to education. Some writers have argued that if the benefits of these programs were counted as additional cash income of recipients, then virtually all families would be lifted out of poverty.[5]

Some of these arguments are overstated since programs like Medicare and Medicaid pay for *extraordinary* medical needs, far above and beyond the typical medical expenses assumed to be included in the official poverty needs standard. A $5,000 Medicaid payment to cover the costs of surgery, for example, merely increases the family's resources by the same amount as the family's needs were increased by the costs of surgery: the net effect on a family's ability to meet its basic needs is virtually unchanged.[6]

However, the argument does hold for one of the largest in-kind benefit programs—the food stamp program. The effects of food stamp "income" on poverty are explored in Chapter 3.

The Official Poverty Line as a Faulty Measure of Needs

Accepting the argument that food needs are a proper basis for a poverty level needs standard, it is easy to argue that the official standard

is unrealistically low. Although generous enough for "nutritional adequacy" as determined by the National Research Council, the food needs
standard was designated as appropriate only for "temporary or emergency use." It assumes that absolutely no meals are eaten outside the
home and also requires considerable sophistication in food purchase and
preparation. Some evidence (Orshansky, 1969) indicates that very few
families whose resources are below the poverty line actually achieve
adequate nutrition. Perhaps the best way of stating this argument is to
ask whether in 1982 a family of four with only $180 per week for food,
housing, and other goods and services could have provided itself with an
adequate standard of living.

It has been argued that a minimal living standard ought not to be
based on food needs but rather on general living standards in the society
as a whole. If nothing else, the concept of poverty is a relative one;
poverty levels of income in the United States might be viewed as very
generous indeed by most developing countries. It follows that the definition of poverty ought to be based not only on changes in the cost of a
fixed bundle of necessities of life but on changes in the composition of
the bundle as well. Survey evidence (Rainwater, 1975) tends to confirm
that the level of income perceived as the minimum needed to get by on
tends to rise not only with inflation but also with increases in real living
standards. An often proposed relative poverty measure is some fraction
(usually one-half) of the nation's median income level. Those convinced
by arguments favoring a relative standard should note that the official
poverty standard has risen only with inflation since it was first developed, and thus has fallen further behind a relative standard.

The Importance of the Accounting Period

The general statement that poverty depends on a comparison of resources and needs does not address the question of the accounting period over which income and needs are measured. The official poverty
definition is based on a comparison of annual family income with annual
needs. A one-year accounting period is convenient, widespread, and, for
many purposes, appropriate in addressing poverty-related issues. For
example, we need to identify families in need of short-term emergency
assistance (such as help with their winter heating bills), since a family
suffering an atypical bad year without financial reserves or the ability to
borrow is as needy as a family in persistently straitened circumstances.
An annual or even shorter accounting period is proper for identifying

families needing short-term emergency relief. However, in targeting longer-run programs, such as those seeking to improve educational opportunities or to provide job training, a one-year accounting period is too short and may misclassify many families.

Perhaps more important, a one-year accounting period may distort our understanding of the causes and consequences of longer-term poverty. The snapshot pictures of the poor provided by annual information from Census Bureau surveys show the characteristics of these individuals who are poor in any one year. If the *persistently* poor are in fact a smaller but *similar* subset of these one-year-poor groups, then the picture painted with Census Bureau data will not be very misleading. But if the characteristics of the one-year and the persistently poor are dissimilar, then not only will the policies directed at longer-term poverty miss the mark by relying on annual poverty information, but so too will efforts to test the various theories of long-term poverty.

The Panel Study provides information on the experiences of a representative sample of families observed over more than a decade. In the next sections, several questions concerning the extent and nature of long-term poverty are addressed using Panel Study data. First, how much turnover is there in the poverty population, and how large is the persistently poor segment of that population? Second, how are these estimates of the extent of poverty affected by raising the poverty line? Third, what are the characteristics of the persistently poor? Finally, Panel Study data are used to investigate the determinants of longer-term poverty: if there is something about these individuals or their environments that leads them to longer-term poverty, can it be identified—and can the condition be corrected?

Throughout the remainder of this chapter, poverty statistics are based on an income measure that includes cash welfare income but omits in-kind welfare income.

Patterns of Annual Poverty

Census Bureau calculations of the incidence of poverty are based on a comparison of a family's annual cash income and the annual needs standard applicable to that family. These comparisons have been made each year by the Census Bureau from its large Current Population Surveys and can be made from the Panel Study data as well. Figure 2.1 plots the path of these one-year snapshot pictures of the extent of poverty.

According to the Census Bureau figures, the incidence of poverty

Figure 2.1

INCIDENCE OF ANNUAL POVERTY IN THE UNITED STATES, CENSUS BUREAU (1960–81) vs. PANEL STUDY (1969–78) DATA

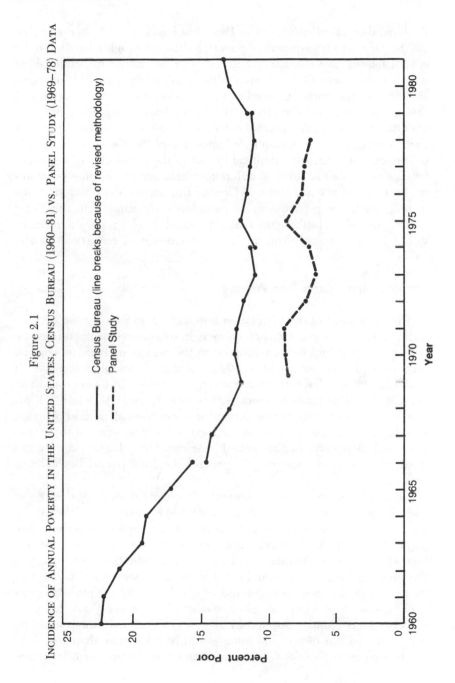

declined dramatically during the 1960s but has changed little during the 1970s. Panel Study estimates of poverty, although roughly parallel to the official figures, are consistently lower. This has raised questions about whether the Panel Study sample is too small or in some way unrepresentative of the national population, but other evidence indicates that this is not the case. The size of the Panel Study sample is more than adequate to obtain fairly precise estimates of the nation's poor.[7] Furthermore, the general demographic composition of the Panel Study sample continues to be virtually identical to that of the population of the country as a whole.[8] One study of differences between the income estimates of the Panel Study and those of Census Bureau surveys concluded that income might be reported more completely by families in the Panel Study, and the resulting increase in Panel Study reported incomes would lead to lower estimates of the incidence of poverty (Minarik, 1975).[9]

Turnover and Longer-Run Poverty

The movement of the population into and out of poverty can be seen in many ways.[10] The most direct way is to estimate what fraction of the poor in a particular year remain poor in the next year. If there were no turnover, this fraction would be 100 percent; with complete turnover, it would be zero. In fact, the fraction ranges from about 54 percent to 65 percent for adjacent-year pairs between 1969 and 1978 (Hill, 1981: p.105). In other words, between one-third and one-half of those who are poor in one year are not poor in the next. Of course, some of those who move out of poverty in the second year may move back in during the third year, so it is important to expand the time period beyond two years.

Table 2.1 presents a more complete picture of the short- and long-run mobility of the poverty population. A single-year estimate of the official poor, shown in the first column, first row, was 6.8 percent of the entire population in 1978. If poverty and nonpoverty were permanent states, then those same individuals, and therefore an identical percentage of the entire population, would be found to have been poor in any and every one of the prior ten years. But if none of the people who were poor in one year were also poor in any of the other years, then 68 percent (6.8 percent multiplied by 10 years) of the population would be poor one year out of ten, but none would be poor more than one year.

The figures in Table 2.1 show a substantial but by no means complete

Table 2.1

INCIDENCE OF SHORT- AND LONG-RUN POVERTY, 1969–1978

	Percent of U.S. Population Poor if Poverty Defined As:	
	Total Money Income Less Than Needs (Official Definition)	Total Money Income Less Than Needs × 1.25
Poor in 1978	6.8%	11.0%
Poor 1 or more years, 1969–78	24.4	32.5
Poor 5 or more years, 1969–1978	5.4	11.0
Poor all 10 years, 1969–78	0.7	2.1
"Persistently poor" (poor 8 or more years, 1969–78)	2.6	5.1

Table reads: "6.8% of the U.S. population was poor in 1978, according to the official definition of poverty, but if the poverty standard were increased 25%, the proportion defined as poor would be increased by more than 50% (to 11% of the U.S. population)."

turnover. About one-quarter (24.4 percent) of the population lived in families with incomes below the official poverty line in at least one of the ten years, 5.4 percent were poor at least five years, and less than one in a hundred (0.7 percent) was poor all ten years.

Persistent poverty can be defined as having income below needs in most or all of the ten years. Surely those individuals poor in *all* of the ten years are persistently poor, but such a definition is unduly restrictive. It omits those who earned or otherwise received enough income to lift them a few dollars above the poverty line in one of the ten years. A more reasonable definition of persistent poverty is being poor *most* of the time. The definition used here is that those who are poor in at least eight of the ten years are *persistently poor.* In terms of this definition, Panel Study data indicate that about 2.6 percent of the population was persistently poor during the 1969-1978 period.[11]

The incidence of short- and long-run poverty is depicted in Figure 2.2, which is based on the experiences of the entire population.[12] As pointed out above, a surprisingly high percentage of the population—24.4 percent—experienced at least some poverty during that decade. For more than half of this group (and for 13.6 percent of the entire population), poverty did not occur more than twice.[13] But one tenth of

Figure 2.2
INCIDENCE OF PERSISTENT POVERTY IN THE UNITED STATES, 1969–1978

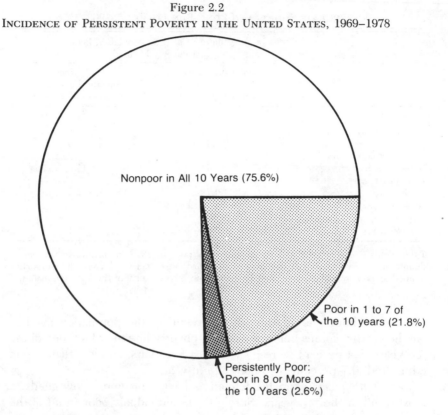

the group (and 2.6 percent of the entire population) was persistently poor. For the remainder (8.3 percent of the entire population) poverty was intermittent, occurring for three to seven of the ten years.

Raising the Poverty Standard

Since many believe that the official poverty standard is too low, it is useful to examine how a 25 percent increase in the needs standard would affect the estimated incidence of short- and long-run poverty. These effects will, of course, depend upon the size and characteristics of the group of individuals with incomes sufficient to place them just above the poverty line.

As shown in the second column of Table 2.1, these effects are dramatic. The incidence of one-year poverty is increased by more than half (from 6.8 percent to 11.0 percent), and the incidence of persistent poverty is nearly doubled (from 2.6 percent to 5.1 percent). This indicates that a substantial proportion of the population lives on the margin of poverty and would be brought into the poverty counts if the needs standard were somewhat increased.[14]

Changes in the Persistence of Long-Run Poverty

Our analysis has found substantial turnover in the poverty population during the 1969–1978 decade, with nearly one-quarter of the population poor at least once, but a very small fraction persistently poor. In looking at the entire decade, we have not yet considered the possibility that the nature of short- and longer-term poverty may have changed. Ideally, we would like to know whether the extent of turnover was as widespread in prior decades. The Panel Study information is limited to the late 1960s and the 1970s, so we are confined to examining this ten-year span for structural changes between the first five-year period (1969–1973) and the second (1974–1978). The economic conditions of these two periods differed substantially. Although there was a recession in the first period, it was mild in comparison with the deep recession during the first two years of the second period. And although single-year inflation was highest in the first period (in 1973, when it reached 11 percent), the overall rise in prices was considerably greater during the second period (32 percent) than during the first period (19 percent).

The results of this analysis are easily summarized: despite different economic conditions and social policies, there were no perceptible changes in the structure of short- and longer-term poverty. A comparison of the first five-year period with the second shows that almost equal fractions of the population were poor in at least one of the five years (17.5 percent in the first period, 16.6 percent in the second). Of these individuals, the fraction poor for one year only or for all five years was virtually identical between the two periods. Finally, there was no trend in the year-to-year poverty turnover rates. Thus, neither the extent of turnover nor the incidence of temporary or persistent poverty appears to have changed within the decade.

What Can Patterns of Poverty Tell Us about its Nature?

Movement into and out of poverty is extensive. Some individuals are poor for only a few years, while a relatively small number are persistently poor for most of the time. Panel Study data provide information on both the patterns of poverty and the characteristics of individuals with different patterns. Before linking patterns with characteristics, we explore the question of whether the year-to-year patterns of poverty themselves can shed light on its causes.

We can illustrate these patterns with information from the five-year period from 1974 to 1978. The fraction of the population that fell below the poverty line varied a bit from one year to the next during this time, ranging from a high of 8.6 percent during the recession year of 1975 to a low of 7.1 percent in the final year.[15] About one-sixth (16.6 percent) of the population was poor in at least one of those five years, while less than two percent (1.8 percent) were poor in every one of those five years.

Suppose we designate individuals who were poor in a given year with a "1" and those who were nonpoor with a "0." Each individual in the population has a five-year pattern of 1's and 0's corresponding to whether he or she was poor in each of the five years. Those who never fell into poverty would have the pattern 00000, those poor in the second year only would be represented as 01000, those poor in all but the last year would show up as 11110, and so on. What can these patterns tell us about the nature of poverty?

First, the patterns illustrate the diversity of experiences with poverty. It might be thought that those experiencing poverty would tend to group themselves into certain characteristic patterns. One might find a group with progressive upward mobility (with patterns like 11000, 11100, etc.), a group with downward mobility (00111, 00011, etc.), and a remainder persistently poor (11111). But this is not the case. There are 32 possible combinations of poverty patterns for this five-year period, and at least a handful of Panel Study individuals fell into each of the 32 patterns. The most frequent pattern, of course, is 00000, representing the five-sixths of the population that escaped poverty altogether. Of the remaining 31, the most frequent pattern was a single-year poverty episode in the recession year of 1975, experienced by only 2 percent of the population. Close behind was the 1.8 percent of the population who were poor in every one of the five years. The only other patterns that were experienced by at least 1 percent of the population were single-year poverty episodes in years other than 1975. In sum, patterns of poverty are quite diverse and refuse to conform to a simple typology.

But we can be more sophisticated in our search for order in these patterns. A crucial question regarding the nature of poverty is whether there is anything about the effects of poverty itself, rather than the personal characteristics of the poor or the effects of their environment, that leads to subsequent poverty. It is certainly true that an individual's chances of being poor "next year" are heavily influenced by whether he or she was poor "this year." The patterns of poverty between 1974 and 1978 reveal that between 50 and 65 percent of the poor in a given year were poor in the next year as well. In contrast, only 3 to 4 percent of those nonpoor in a given year were poor the next.

Although these differences are suggestive, they do not prove that it is prior poverty *as such* that causes the subsequent poverty. The true causes of persistent poverty may instead be found in unchanging characteristics of poor individuals or their environments—for example, education, sex, marital status of the family head, or geographic location. We can examine the five-year patterns more closely to distinguish between these two possibilities. To look at patterns evidenced by people who experienced poverty in at least two out of five years, suppose we take all of the individuals who were poor in both 1974 and in one of the other years. Four patterns are possible: 11000, 10100, 10010, and 10001. If poverty as such—rather than other personal and environmental factors—is itself the cause of subsequent poverty, then most of the individuals' patterns should take the 11000 form, indicating that poverty episodes tend to be self-perpetuating. But if individuals' poverty episodes are more evenly spread over all four possible patterns, then factors other than poverty itself would appear to play the stronger causal role.

Using a recently developed analytic technique to investigate these patterns, Hill (1981) found that while there was a modest tendency for poverty episodes to lump themselves together, most were in fact dispersed intermittently throughout the period, indicating a very loose relationship between prior and subsequent poverty and an important role for some other unchanging characteristics in the lives of those who were poor at some time during the period.[16]

Explaining Short- and Long-Run Poverty

Poverty has been defined as a state in which resources are insufficient to meet basic needs. In turn, the definition of basic needs is primarily a function of family size and society's judgment about what constitutes a minimal living standard for families of different sizes, while the definition of resources is primarily a function of the cash income and noncash (in-kind) benefits received by family members.

A complete explanation of why individuals are poor would require many interrelated parts. An understanding of family composition differences requires theories of marriage, divorce, and fertility. The definition of what constitutes minimal living standards requires an understanding of society's judgments of basic needs and how they change over time. Since most of a family's income comes from the labor market, we also need to know the determinants of the wage rate an individual can command for each hour worked, and understand how many hours, if any, each individual chooses or is constrained (through unemployment or underemployment) to work. Since some income is a return on savings or other assets, we need to explain why some individuals accumulate such assets and others do not. Finally, since some income comes as transfers from the government, we need to know why these various transfer programs exist, how generous they are, and why some eligible individuals do not participate in them. Compounding our task, these explanations must take family decisions, rather than individual decisions, as their base. Moreover, these components are obviously interrelated. Of particular policy concern is how transfer programs affect decisions about work hours, savings, childbearing, marriage, and divorce.

Although it is important to know how many of the poor are elderly or disabled, most theories of poverty focus on able-bodied, nonelderly adults, whose potential for rising out of poverty rests on their ability to work enough hours at a sufficiently high wage rate. Such theories of poverty consequently become theories of wage rates and labor supply. Schiller (1976) groups such explanations into categories of "flawed character" and "restricted opportunity." The "character" explanation assumes that there are abundant opportunities for improving one's economic status, but that the poor fail to take advantage of them because of lack of initiative and diligence. The "opportunity" explanations, on the other hand, contend that the poor have been denied sufficient access to economic opportunities and that, regardless of their initiative or diligence, they cannot avoid poverty unless their economic opportunities improve.

Foremost among the character explanations is Oscar Lewis's "culture of poverty" theory. Developed from anthropological case studies of poor families in a number of countries, this theory was influential in formulating policies to fight the war on poverty. The theory holds that an identifiable minority of poor families share attitudes and values that keep them poor and cause poverty to be passed on to their children as well:

Once it [the culture of poverty] comes into existence, it tends to perpetuate itself from generation to generation because of its effects on children. By the time slum children are age six or seven, they have usually absorbed the basic values and attitudes of their subculture and are not psychologically geared to take full advantage of changing conditions or increased opportunities which may occur in their lifetime (Lewis, 1968: p. 50).

In other words, Lewis thinks poverty is more a function of the way people think than of their physical environment, and thus to cure poverty one would have to change the attitudes of the poor. Lewis does not believe that all of the poor share in this culture of poverty; rather, he offers a "rough guess . . . that only about 20 percent of the population below the poverty line . . . in the United States have characteristics which would justify classifying their way of life as that of a culture of poverty" (Lewis, 1968: p. 57). The poverty Lewis describes is persistent—lasting many years and even spanning generations. Since the Panel Study was designed to include measures of some of the attitudes thought to be part of the culture of poverty, we will be able to test whether they differentiate the long-term poor from others.

The conventional economic approach to poverty is to regard it as a problem of low individual productivity. The ideological foundation for this view is the human capital theory, developed in its modern form by Becker (1975). A more detailed explanation of this theory is given in Chapter 4, but it is sufficient here to note that it views an individual's productivity as dependent upon the training acquired formally, as through school, or through less formal on-the-job training. Although the acquisition and monetary value of this training may be influenced by discrimination, nepotism, and changing labor market opportunities, the focus of the human capital approach is on the productivity of the individual.

Other theories shift the focus away from the individual to the labor market in which he or she works. The labor markets in which low-wage workers find themselves are seen as characterized by instability and little chance for advancement; indeed, career ladders may be lacking entirely. Furthermore, the dynamics of these labor markets are seen as causing workers to develop working habits that tend to lock them into their jobs and greatly reduce their chances of moving into the more stable, better-paid labor market. In this view, low-wage employment is not a result of individual productivity but rather is a result of the structure of the labor market in which low-wage workers are employed. This is clearly a "restricted opportunity" view of poverty.

The multitude of factors affecting economic well-being makes a simple, single "test" of the various theories of poverty impossible. Instead, we will begin with a descriptive overview of the characteristics of the persistently poor, followed by an explicit examination of the role of work hours, unemployment, and low wage rates as possible causes of poverty, and finally, we will look at the factors associated with changes in poverty status. This analysis parallels the general analysis in Chapter 1 of the ways in which attitudes, other background factors, and events operate to produce changes in the economic status of a group of households representative of the entire population, but differs from it by focusing on initially poor male and female heads of households.

Characteristics of the Short- and Longer-Term Poor

If we had found little turnover in the poverty population, differences in the characteristics of the short- and long-term poor would not be of concern, and the use of a one-year accounting period would not have misclassified many of the poor. An understanding of the incidence of one-year poverty would have been equivalent to an understanding of longer-term poverty. But the Panel Study data show considerable turnover, with a substantial number of individuals who are only intermittently poor, and a much smaller group who are persistently poor. When we examine the demographic characteristics of these different groups, we find striking differences between the characteristics of the persistently poor and those only temporarily poor during the decade, and notable differences between the characteristics of those two groups together and those of the group of individuals poor in a specific year (1978). The temporarily poor do not appear to be very different from the population as a whole, appearing to differ from nonpoor families only in that they have one or two bad years. In contrast, the persistently poor are heavily concentrated into two overlapping groups: black households and female-headed households.

Table 2.2 compares the demographic characteristics of individuals poor in one year (1978), individuals poor only one or two years out of the ten from 1969 through 1978 (termed here the "temporarily poor"), and individuals poor at least eight out of the ten years (the persistently poor). For purposes of comparison, the demographic composition of the *entire* population (not just the poor) is given in the final column.[17] Although the table is based on counts of *individuals* poor in the various time periods, many of the demographic characteristics relate to the head of the household in which the individual resided in 1978.

Table 2.2

DEMOGRAPHIC CHARACTERISTICS OF THE ONE-YEAR POOR, PERSISTENTLY POOR, AND TEMPORARILY POOR, 1969–1978

Demographic Characteristics Of Household Heads, 1978	Poor in 1978	Persistently Poor (8 or More Years, 1969–78)	Temporarily Poor (1 or 2 Years, 1969–78)	Entire U.S. Population
All Females	59%	61%	28%	19%
Elderly	13	18	7	5
Nonelderly				
White	22	13	16	10
Black	25	31	6	4
All Males	42	39	73	80
Elderly	10	15	7	8
Nonelderly				
White	21	4	54	65
Black	11	20	11	6
Rural (town of 10,000 or less)	21	33	19	15
Urban (city of 500,000 or more)	26	21	33	33
Southern U.S.	46	68	30	30
Disabled	31	39	17	11
Black	42	62	19	12
Number of observations	2,247	990	2,041	15,753
Estimated fraction of U.S. population in each group	7.2%	2.2%	13.6%	100.0%

Table reads: "Almost three-fifths (59%) of all individuals poor in 1978 lived in families headed by a woman. Of the entire population in 1978, less than one-fifth (19%) lived in families headed by a woman."

The following can serve to illustrate the structure of Table 2.2. In the rightmost column ("Entire Population") the numeral 6 appears in the eighth row down, showing that of the entire population, only 6 percent lived in families headed by a black man under the age of 65.[18] Relative to this 6 percent figure for the entire population, individuals living in such families are overrepresented among both the one-year poor (11 percent) and the temporarily poor (11 percent) and are particularly overrepresented among the persistently poor (20 percent). Thus, persistent poverty is considerably more concentrated among households headed by nonelderly black men than the one-year poverty figures would indicate.

In general, the demographic composition of the temporarily poor is much more similar to the composition of the population as a whole than it is to that of the persistently poor or to those found to be poor in a given year.[19] Whereas 5 percent of the entire population lived in families headed by an elderly woman, 7 percent of the temporarily poor were in such a situation. Comparable fractions were also found for families headed by an elderly man. The geographic location of both groups was similar as well. The temporarily poor were somewhat more likely to be black or to live in a household headed by a woman or a disabled individual, but these differences were small relative to the sharply different characteristics of the persistently poor.

A glance at the second column of figures in Table 2.2 reveals that the characteristics of the persistently poor differ substantially from all other groups, including the one-year poor. Persistent poverty is heavily concentrated among blacks, and particularly among families headed by a black woman. Although blacks constitute only about 12 percent of the entire population and 42 percent of the one-year poor, they account for 62 percent of the persistently poor. Almost as striking is the concentration of persistent poverty among families headed by a woman. Although just one-fifth (19 percent) of the entire population lived in such families, they accounted for more than three-fifths (61 percent) of the persistently poor. But while similar proportions of the one-year poor and the persistently poor were living in households headed by a woman, these proportions differed markedly by race. Of the individuals poor in 1978, almost one-half (47 percent) lived in households headed by nonelderly women; slightly over half of these female household heads were black and slightly less than half were white. Of the persistently poor individuals, roughly half also lived in households headed by women, but persistent poverty was much more heavily concentrated among families headed by black women than among those headed by white women—indeed, nearly one-third (31 percent) of all of the persistently poor (in contrast to 25 percent of those poor in 1978) were found to be living in families headed by a nonelderly black woman.

A comparable racial difference shows up for male-headed families. In the population as a whole, individuals living in families headed by nonelderly white men (65 percent) outnumbered those in families headed by nonelderly black men (6 percent) by 10 to 1. But among the persistently poor, the ratio actually reverses to 1 to 5, with only 4 percent of the persistently poor living in families headed by nonelderly white men as compared with 20 percent in families headed by nonelderly black men.

Poverty figures from a single year also give a misleading picture of the location of the persistently poor. Whereas more of the one-year poor lived in large urban areas than in small towns or rural areas, the proportion of the persistently poor living in large urban areas is considerably smaller than the comparable fraction living in small towns or rural areas. Taken together, the figures shown in Table 2.2 concerning the location of poverty suggest that southern and rural poverty are much more persistent than is urban poverty. These findings do not support Lewis' (1968) emphasis on northern, urban blacks nor Auletta's (1982) depiction of the persistently poor as an urban underclass. Although persistent poverty is heavily concentrated among blacks (and their poverty may well be explained by factors unrelated to their culture), it is not heavily concentrated in northern urban areas. Among the persistently poor, only about one-fifth lived in cities of 500,000 or more, a smaller proportion than of the one-year poor or even of the population as a whole. Despite the fact that the official poverty standards were lower for farm families than for nonfarm families during the 1970s, rural poverty appears to be more persistent than urban poverty, characterizing about one-third of the persistently poor.

Finally, it must be noted that the poverty counts discussed in this section include cash welfare payments in the measure of income. Excluding those payments not only increases the number of families found to be poor "prewelfare," but also results in a somewhat different geographic distribution for the prewelfare persistently poor. Long-term welfare payments are concentrated among families living in urban areas, so subtracting welfare from income results in a percentage of those living in large cities which is as high among the prewelfare persistently poor as in the population as a whole. Characteristics of the prewelfare poor are given in Table 2.3. A more complete discussion of welfare and poverty is given in Chapter 3.

Table 2.3

DEMOGRAPHIC CHARACTERISTICS OF PREWELFARE ONE-YEAR POOR, PERSISTENTLY POOR, AND TEMPORARILY POOR, 1969–1978

Demographic Characteristics of Household Heads, 1978	Poor in 1978	Persistently Poor (8 or more years, 1969–78)	Temporarily Poor (1 or 2 years, 1969–78)	Entire U.S. Population
All Females	62%	62%	26%	19%
Elderly	13	15	6	5
Nonelderly				
White	24	14	16	10
Black	25	33	4	4
All Males	38	38	75	80
Elderly	8	12	7	8
Nonelderly				
White	21	10	58	65
Black	9	16	10	6
Rural (town of 10,000 or less)	19	24	20	15
Urban (city of 500,000 or more)	30	33	32	33
Southern U.S.	40	50	31	30
Disabled	31	41	15	11
Black	41	58	15	12
Number of observations	2,709	1,509	1,876	15,753
Estimated fraction of entire population in group	9.0%	3.8%	11.6%	100.0%

Table reads: "Over three-fifths (62%) of individuals whose 1978 family income excluding cash welfare payments was less than poverty needs lived in families headed by a woman. Of the entire U.S. population in 1978, less than one-fifth (19%) lived in families headed by a woman."

Work Hours, Wage Rates, and Poverty

For households headed by able-bodied individuals, earned income is viewed as the best vehicle for climbing out or staying out of poverty. Labor income is the product of two components—the hourly pay rate and the total number of hours worked. In this section, we explore the relationship between work hours, wages, and poverty, and assess the influence of abnormally low wages or few work hours on the poverty status of families.

Most of the group that we have defined as persistently poor lived in households where the head worked in fewer than half of the ten years under study. Thus it would appear that employment offers considerable potential for raising some of the persistently poor out of poverty. But a closer look at the persistently poor reveals that the vast majority live in households headed by someone who might not be expected to work because of a physical or mental disability, age, or childcare responsibilities. In fact, only about one-sixth of the persistently poor live in households headed by an able-bodied, prime-age man, and nearly half of these men worked for substantial periods in at least five of the ten years.

To what extent can the economic status of families headed by able-bodied, nonelderly men and women be improved through increased work hours or higher wages? Levy (1976) calculated answers to two "what if" questions in order to determine the effects of low numbers of work hours and low wage rates among Panel Study households headed by able-bodied individuals for the years 1967 and 1972.[20] His results are discussed in the following sections.

Effects of Low Work Hours and Unemployment

What if the heads of poor households all had full-time jobs at their reported hourly wage rates?[21] Levy found that low numbers of work hours were not a major factor in the incidence of poverty among households headed by either men or women. The typical able-bodied, nonelderly male household head living below the poverty line worked 85 percent of normal full-time work hours, and increasing work hours to 100 percent would have lifted very few out of poverty. Female household heads in poverty, on the other hand, did work many fewer hours than their nonpoor counterparts. However, their wage rates were so low that even large increases in work hours would not have pulled many of them above the poverty line.

This weak relationship between low work hours and poverty was borne out by an examination of poverty and unemployment undertaken by Corcoran and Hill (1980). They used Panel Study information for the years between 1967 and 1975 to calculate the fraction of the poverty population that would not have been poor if the heads of their households had been able to work the amount of time they reported being unemployed. Overall, the heads of poor households were unemployed for less than three weeks per year, losing an average of about $620 annually.[22] Unemployment compensation made up for only about one-sixth of these lost earnings. The addition of earnings lost because of unemployment would have brought only about one-tenth of all individuals in poor households out of poverty. Clearly, then, low numbers of work hours in general and unemployment in particular were not a predominant cause of poverty among the households headed by nonelderly, able-bodied individuals.

Effects of Low Wage Rates

What if heads of poor households had worked their reported number of hours at "normal" wage rates? The concept of "normal" wage rates is more complicated than "normal" work hours. The latter can be reasonably assumed to be equal to the overall average, full-time work week. But it would not be reasonable to assume that all heads of poor households could earn a pay rate equal to the overall average since hourly earnings are systematically related to the demographic characteristics that distinguish the heads of poor and nonpoor households—level of education, geographic location, race, sex, and so forth. Thus a more appropriate procedure is to define "normal" pay rates as the average hourly earnings of individuals with similar characteristics. Levy finds that based on the characteristics of the heads of poor households the *expected* average wage rates were very low—between $2.00 and $2.20 per hour in 1967 for all men and for white women, and only about $1.30 per hour for black women.[23] Low as these expected wage rates were, the actual wage rates of these men and women were still lower—between 10 and 40 percent less than the expected rates. If wage rates of poor household heads had been brought up to the expected "normal" level, while maintaining the same number of work hours, the incidence of poverty among male-headed households would have declined by 30 to 40 percent. For women, on the other hand, the increase in wage rates from the actual to the expected "normal" would not have increased labor incomes sufficiently to bring many of the households headed by a woman out of poverty.

In sum, poverty among female household heads is neither a function of an abnormally low number of work hours nor of wage rates that are abnormally low for women with similar characteristics. Normal wage rates of women with comparable demographic traits would be too low to bring many of the poor female heads out of poverty. Neither low work hours in general nor unemployment in particular keep many households headed by men below the poverty line.[24] Most of these able-bodied men work close to full time, and while a relatively small number do suffer long spells of unemployment, only a small number would be lifted out of poverty if unemployment were completely eliminated. Poverty among male household heads is much more a function of unusually low wage rates. Although the problem may be due in part to temporary misfortunes that occur occasionally and randomly, it may also stem from permanent characteristics of some men that lead to lower wages. In the next section we examine in more detail the role of personal characteristics, labor market experience, and marital status in improving the long-run economic well-being of poor families.

What Causes Some of the Poor to Improve Their Status?

We have seen the dramatic extent of turnover in the poverty population, indicating that many of those who were poor at one time subsequently escape from poverty, while a minority suffer from persistent poverty. This diversity of experience provides an opportunity to investigate the initial conditions and subsequent events that distinguish those who do well from those who do not. The analysis presented here parallels that summarized in Chapter 1, except that the unit of analysis here is the family head rather than all individuals. From the entire set of Panel Study families, we selected families that began the 1970s below or near the official poverty line and that were headed by a nondisabled, nonelderly man or woman.[25] Improvements in economic status are measured by increases in the ratio of family income to needs. The measure used here is identical to the one used in Chapter 1—an average annual growth rate in family income/needs during the period from 1971 to 1978.[26]

All in all, the growth in this measure of economic well-being was even more favorable for these initially poor families than for the population as a whole. For more than 75 percent of the male-headed families, the income-to-needs ratios grew faster than inflation, compared with about 70 percent for the female-headed families. Black female household

Table 2.4

INCIDENCE AND EFFECTS OF VARIOUS EVENTS ON GROWTH IN INCOME/NEEDS
FOR INITIALLY POOR HOUSEHOLDS, 1971–1978

| Event | Male Household Heads (Married or Unmarried) | |
	Fraction Experiencing Event	Effect of Event on Annual Growth Rate
Marriage:		
Not married in 1971 married in 1978	8%	*
Labor Force:		
Head worked in both 1971 & 1978	89	*
Head started working	5	+5% higher growth than reference group (below)
Head stopped working	5	*
Head didn't work either time	1	Reference group
Wife worked in both 1971 & 1978	8	*
Wife started working	34	+5% higher growth than reference group (below)
Wife stopped working	8	*
Wife didn't work either time or no wife present	50	Reference group
Children:		
Number of births		2% lower growth per birth
Number of years in which children left home		1% higher growth

heads were somewhat less able to keep pace with inflation than were male and white female household heads, but even among this group, more than 60 percent succeeded in keeping up. As with the averages for the entire population, these figures conceal a great diversity of experience; some families greatly increased their economic well-being while others ended up considerably worse off than they had been originally.

In order to differentiate the successful from the unsuccessful, we used a framework similar to that used for the analysis presented in Chapter 1, distinguishing the effects of initial characteristics such as attitudes, education, and age from events like changes in marital status and movements into and out of the labor force. The events are listed in Table 2.4,

Table 2.4 (Continued)

Event	Female Household Heads (All Unmarried, 1971)		
	Fraction Experiencing Event		Effect of Event on Annual Growth Rate
	White	Black	
Marriage:			
Not married in 1971, married in 1978	41%	14%	+7% higher growth rate than those remaining unmarried
Labor Force:			
Head worked in both 1971 & 1978	38	34	+6% higher growth than reference group (below)
Head started working	31	26	+5% higher growth than reference group (below)
Head stopped working	14	11	−5% lower growth than reference group (below)
Head didn't work either time	17	29	Reference group
Children:			
Number of births		*	
Number of years in which children left home			2% lower growth

Table reads: "Of all white female household heads (unmarried) who were initially poor, 41% had become married in 1978. Of all black female household heads who were initially poor, 14% were married in 1978. Combining the two groups, those who married experienced a 7% higher annual growth rate in income/needs than did those who remained unmarried."

Note: Asterisk (*) indicates that the effect was not statistically significant.

along with their frequency of occurrence and their effects on change in economic status.[27]

By far the most important event for the economic status of female household heads was marriage. All of these women were unmarried in the first year of the period—that is, they had become divorced or separated from a previous marriage, had never been married before, or (in rare cases for these relatively young women) had become widowed. Those who had married by the end of the period had annual income/ needs growth rates that were about seven percentage points higher than for those who had not married.[28] Although 7 percent may seem insignificant, in fact such an increase is quite large, lifting a family just at the poverty line in 1971 to more than 60 percent above it in 1978. There were dramatic differences, however, in the fractions of white and black female household heads who had married. More than two-fifths of the white women had married by 1978, compared with less than one-sixth of the black women. Thus, one main reason that persistent poverty is so much more prevalent among black than white women lies in their differing rates of marriage.

In contrast, neither marriage nor divorce had much effect on the economic status of male household heads. Fewer than one-tenth of these men were unmarried at the beginning and at the end of the period, and their change in economic well-being did not differ significantly from that of comparable men with other marital patterns.

Movements into and out of the labor force might be expected to produce substantial change in economic status, and this was indeed found to be the case, especially for female household heads. Compared with the group of female heads who were out of the labor force at both the beginning (1971) and the end (1978) of the period, those entering the labor force did substantially better, and those leaving it did substantially worse.[29] Perhaps surprisingly, the women who had been working at both points in time and had begun at a higher income level also had the highest income/needs growth rates—6 percent higher, on average, than the reference group composed of those out of the labor force in both 1971 and 1978.

For the male household head, growth in economic status was significantly enhanced if either he or his wife entered the labor force. Note, however, that the vast majority (89 percent) of these able-bodied men under the age of 45 were working at both points in time.

Other demographic events also had some effects. Births were associated with lower income/needs growth rates in households headed by men, presumably because births reduce the work hours of wives and increase family needs. The effects of births were not strong enough to be statistically significant for households headed initially by women. Children leaving home had a significant effect on both groups, but with contrasting results. For male-headed families, children who left had consumed more than they had earned so their departure had a positive net effect on the growth in income/needs. The reverse was true for female-headed families—the net result of their children's departure was to take away more in income than they had consumed and thus lower the growth in well-being of the family left behind.

As a second step in the analysis, we attempted to distinguish success-

ful from unsuccessful households by using a set of characteristics measured in the initial years, including race, attitudes, age, and education.
Here the results differed substantially for the female and male household heads, and each group is discussed in turn.[30]

Race was one of the most powerful predictors of which of the initially
poor female household heads would do better in subsequent years, with
white women enjoying annual growth rates in income/needs that were
about four percentage points higher than those of black women. This
effect was estimated using a statistical procedure that made adjustments
for differences in age, education, attitudes, and initial level of income/
needs, so the racial differences could not be attributed to differences in
any of these characteristics.[31] An investigation of the role of race in the
various events confirmed the importance of marriage in producing this
difference; more than half of the race difference could be attributed to
the lower incidence of marriage among black female heads of households. None of the other events accounted for a significant share of this
racial effect.

Analysts have made repeated attempts to test whether the attitudinal
measures were capable of identifying the initially low-income families
who would do better subsequently. Morgan made the first and in some
respects most thorough attempt, and he summarizes his findings, based
on five years of information, in the following way: "[O]ur search for
possible individual attitudes and behavior patterns . . . that may affect
family status . . . [showed that] . . . nothing individuals believe or do
has an effect that persists consistently through the different statistical
procedures and measures" (Morgan, 1974: p. 75). Two years later he
reached the same conclusion from his analyses of seven years of data
(Morgan, 1976).

In the present analysis, there was some evidence that women with
higher initial levels of achievement motivation were subsequently more
successful, primarily because of increased chances of labor force entry
and decreased chances of leaving the labor force, but many of these
estimated effects were on the borderline of statistical significance. The
effects of efficacy on income/needs growth were also positive but not
statistically significant at conventional levels. The effect of the other
attitudinal measure, future orientation, was negative but insignificant.[32]

These initial characteristics were considerably less able to differentiate successful and unsuccessful male household heads. Black men had
growth rates in income/needs that were about three percentage points
lower than for whites, but these differences were only at the margin of

statistical significance. Those with higher levels of education did somewhat better; the growth rates of high school graduates were about two
percent higher than the growth rates of those with only an eighth grade
education. Attitude differences failed to account for high and low growth
rates.

Summary

The Panel Study's decade-long survey of poverty shows that the
popular conception of "the poor" as a homogeneous, stable group is
simply wrong. Although the series of snapshot pictures of poverty provided by the Census Bureau surveys show fairly constant numbers and
characteristics for poor families each year, actual turnover in the poverty
population is very high. Only about two-thirds of the individuals living
in families with cash incomes below the poverty line in a given year
were still poor in the following year, and only about one-third of the
poor in a given year were poor for at least eight of the ten prior years.
Although the living standard afforded by a poverty level income may be
unrealistically low, and although many individuals climbing out of poverty may not go very far, it is clear that persistent poverty characterizes
a considerably smaller fraction of our population than the one-year figures would suggest. The addition of in-kind (noncash) benefits from the
government would decrease the estimates of persistent poverty still further, although the effects on poverty of programs that assist families
having extraordinary (e.g., medical) needs can be overstated.

The flip side of the turnover coin is that poverty touched the lives of a
surprisingly large fraction of the population over a ten-year period.
About one-quarter of the population was found to have lived in poor
families in at least one of the ten years between 1969 and 1978, but for
half of this group, poverty years did not occur more than twice. Very
few characteristics distinguished those individuals from the population
as a whole. They were somewhat more likely to be black or to live in
families headed by a woman, but on the whole, the main difference
between them and the rest of the population was simply that they had
experienced one or two particularly bad years.

In contrast, the characteristics of the persistently poor were quite
different from those of the population as a whole and even differed from
the characteristics of individuals found to be poor in a given year. The
single most powerful factor that distinguished persistently poor people
from the poor in a given year was race—more than three-fifths of the

persistently poor were black. Although it has long been known that the incidence of annual poverty is considerably higher among black families than white, the Panel Study information, spanning more than a decade, reveals that blacks are even more disproportionately represented among the persistently poor than among the poor in a given year. The effects of race were particularly strong for families headed by a woman, and could not be attributed to differences in such characteristics as education or attitudes.

Although the economic fortunes of many low-income individuals fluctuate a great deal from one year to the next, it was possible to identify some who had improved their economic status. For low-income women who headed their own households, marriage was the most important factor associated with increased economic well-being. This improvement held true for both white and black women, but marriage itself was much more frequent among white women. For men who headed low-income families, changes in marital status did not significantly affect economic status. And, finally, there was no evidence that the initial attitudes of male household heads affected their subsequent improvement in economic status, and there was little evidence of such effects for female household heads.

Implications

Findings from the Panel Study show, most importantly, that it is crucial to distinguish between those who fall into relatively brief periods of poverty and those who are unable to meet basic needs for prolonged periods. The characteristics of the temporarily poor are similar to those of the population as a whole—there appears to be virtually no demographic attribute that distinguishes people with brief contact with poverty from the rest of society. The implication is that few people are immune to such events as personal illness, adverse local or national economic conditions, or the death or departure of a spouse; and for a substantial proportion, these events can precipitate a year or two of severe hardship. For them, antipoverty programs are perhaps best viewed as insurance programs, available if necessary to cushion them against the most severe impacts of their temporary misfortune. Given time to adjust, they will be able to move out of poverty on an essentially permanent basis, and will presumably be paying taxes to support the very programs that once aided them. The majority of these people escape from temporary poverty in the same ways that most people avoid

entering poverty: by acquiring a job with decent pay or marrying someone who has one.

Less than 3 percent of the population were members of the group we
defined as persistently poor. Although government programs aimed at
fulfilling short-term needs (e.g., help in paying energy bills) need not
distinguish between the shorter- and longer-term poor, programs aimed
at curing longer-term poverty clearly do need to make that distinction.
One type of program allocates aid to state and local units of government
based on the economic status of the population—for example, grants to
school districts, based on annual poverty counts in the counties containing those districts.[33] But other programs, including Federal Revenue
Sharing, use income levels as a criterion in allocating their funds, and
their definitions of poverty are typically based on an annual accounting
period. If we had found that the persistently poor were a similar but
merely smaller subset of the one-year poor, then the use of the one-year
accounting period would not be misleading. However, we found that the
characteristics of the persistently poor differed markedly from those of
the one-year poor, suggesting that allocations based on one-year figures
are not efficiently targeted to reach the longer-term poor. In particular,
for rural areas, the South, and especially areas with heavy concentra-
tions of blacks, allocations based on one-year figures are lower than
warranted by the longer-term poverty prevalent in these areas.

Most antipoverty programs allocate aid to families and individuals,
rather than to school districts or states, and these too need to be formulated with an understanding of the extent and nature of longer-term
poverty. The demographic characteristics of the persistently poor provide some clues about the nature of long-term poverty and have implications for possible policies to combat it.

One-third of the persistently poor are elderly people, who have se-
verely limited opportunities to escape from poverty through either of the
two most common strategies—by acquiring a job with decent pay or
marrying someone who has one. Thus it is not surprising to discover that
the elderly, regardless of race or sex, are disproportionately represented
among the persistently poor. Of course, persistent poverty is not a characteristic of the majority of the elderly. A thorough understanding of why a
certain group of the elderly spend their last years in continual poverty
requires long-term information—as yet unavailable—on their working
lives and past family situations. But given the existence of a group of
persistently poor elderly people, the only apparent method for eliminating such hardship is to provide direct public transfers. In the past decade

major advances in this direction have been undertaken with the liberal-
ization of Social Security eligibility requirements and benefit levels and
the introduction of the Supplemental Security Income (SSI) program.
These reforms have undoubtedly reduced the number of elderly people
who live in long-term poverty. But the Social Security program does not
cover all of the elderly, and the effectiveness of the SSI program has been
weakened by low participation rates among those eligible as well as by the
fact that benefit levels are insufficient in themselves to remove the elderly
from poverty. Increases in benefit levels and better delivery of these
benefits to the elderly appear to be the only short-term policy to eliminate persistent poverty among this group.

Of the remaining two-thirds of the persistently poor—those who are
not elderly—65 percent live in households headed by women, and almost three-quarters of these women are black. Most of the women in
this group have children at home, a fact that has two-fold implications
for the nature of their poverty. Children not only increase the household's needs for income but impose child-care responsibilities that se-
verely constrain the single parent's ability to work full time. Although
public opinion concerning the competing demands of child care and
employment appears to be changing as more women enter the labor
force, it is still not clear whether as a matter of policy mothers should be
encouraged to entrust their children to the care of others so that they
can work.

Unfortunately, even if more child care were provided to help single
parents balance child-care responsibilities with full-time employment,
the available evidence indicates that these women are unlikely to find
jobs paying enough to remove them from poverty. Whether low wage
rates for women are a result of low productivity or some institutional
factor, such as pure discrimination, is an issue of considerable debate.
Evidence detailed in Chapter 6 indicates that a substantial part of the
wage gap between women and white men cannot be attributed to differences in conventional measures of productivity, implying a considerable
role for institutional factors. If this is true, then labor market solutions to
the persistent poverty of women who head their own households would
have to be far-ranging indeed, encompassing more than the traditional
productivity-enhancing manpower [sic] training programs (whose record
of success has not been encouraging). Antipoverty programs would have
to aim at restructuring the basic institutional arrangements of the labor
market, surely a difficult task.

Another common avenue for women to escape persistent poverty is to marry or otherwise combine households with a man whose income (either alone or combined with the woman's income) is sufficient to meet basic needs. The evidence indicates that this route is often taken by white women, but not by black women. The fact that black men are also disproportionately poor lessens the black woman's opportunities for marriage to someone whose income would lift the household out of poverty. In any event, it would not seem appropriate for public policy to exert any active influence on fundamentally private decisions regarding one's living arrangements. The major role of policy with respect to family composition should be no more than to avoid either inadvertently discouraging marriage or remarriage, or encouraging marital dissolution.

One possible long-range approach to preventing long-term poverty before it occurs is to prevent unwanted pregnancies by providing increased birth control information and sexual guidance. Unfortunately, the relevant programs initiated to date do not appear to have been particularly successful. Moreover, certainly not all births in this group were "unwanted," let alone unplanned. Marriage itself, after all, can result in unwanted outcomes of divorce or separation, usually leaving children in female-headed households. Stricter child-support enforcement laws designed to collect from an able father a more substantial amount of the cost of raising his children are one possibility. But past efforts in this direction have been only marginally successful, and because of the typically low incomes of black men, have had virtually no effect on the situation of black women. All in all, one is left with the disheartening conclusion that, as with the elderly, direct public transfers offer the most feasible solution to the difficult problem of persistent poverty among nonelderly female-headed households with children.

Very few nonelderly white men are persistently poor, a fact that presumably reflects their more favorable labor market opportunities. The situation is different for nonelderly black men, who account for a substantial portion of the persistently poor. The possibility of labor market solutions—in particular, programs aimed at raising wage rates—seems most promising for these groups of nonelderly men. The evidence suggests that most individuals in these groups work when jobs are available, but receive abnormally low wages. If they could earn wages normal for persons with similar characteristics, the chances are good that the burden of poverty could be lifted from them. Thus, wage subsidy programs or other programs aimed at increasing their wages, including programs to eliminate racial discrimination in the labor market, appear to be desirable approaches to eliminating the persistent poverty of this group.

A final set of implications of our findings on longer-term poverty concern the efficacy of programs based on the notion of a culture of poverty. Can poverty be eliminated if we change the way poor people think? The relationship between individuals' attitudes and their economic status is a complicated one, and calls for further research, but we see little need to change the qualifications and conclusions reached by Morgan and others after the first five years of the Panel Study project:

> Can one really assert that because we find little evidence that individual attitudes and behavior patterns affect individual economic progress, that massive changes in those attitudes and behaviors would have no effect? Of course we cannot. . . .
>
> Perhaps there has not been enough time for attitudes and behavior patterns to exert their effects over inertia, random fluctuations, and sluggish aggregate economic conditions. Perhaps we have not measured the right things or have not measured them well enough. Perhaps we have not adequately isolated the autonomous groups for whom individual factors can show their effects and not be dominated by other factors.
>
> On the other hand, we may have been oversold on the Protestant Ethic and have refused to see the extent to which people are the victims of their past, their environment, luck, and chance.
>
> It is after all difficult to believe that there are not some situations where individual effort matters—in seizing opportunities for better jobs, moving to new areas, or avoiding undue risks. But for public policy purposes and for arguments about the extent to which one could reduce dependency in our society by changing the behavior and attitudes of dependent members, the findings certainly do not encourage expectations that such changes would make much difference (Morgan et al., 1974, p. 366).

Notes

[1]For a review of the development of the official poverty standard and its competitors, see U.S. Department of Health, Education, and Welfare (1976).

[2]Some would dispute this definition and argue that poverty depends not only on the level of resources but the way in which they are used to provide a standard of living. See, for example, Rainwater (1975) and Townsend (1979).

[3]Among the several different food cost estimates (descriptively titled "thrifty," "low cost," "moderate cost," and "liberal"), the most parsimonious, "thrifty" plan, is used as a basis for the official standard. Examples of these estimates of weekly food needs in March 1980 were: $14.80 for a 20- to 54-year-old man, $12.10 for a 20- to 54-year-old woman, and $6.70 for a child under the age of 3. Food needs are summed for all family members and multiplied by 52 to obtain an estimate of annual food needs. To go from food needs to total needs, the former are multiplied by a factor of roughly 3. The justification for this is that information on expenditures of low-income families show that, on average, roughly one-

third of their income is spent on food. A number of other adjustments are made, the most important of which are downward adjustments for larger families because they enjoy "economies of scale"; that is, many fixed living expenses such as those for heat do not increase proportionately with an increase in family size. The opposite adjustment is made for very small families. Until 1980, the needs of farm families were assumed to be 80 percent of those of otherwise comparable nonfarm families. The official poverty thresholds are listed in Census Bureau publications entitled "Characteristics of the Population Below the Poverty Level," Current Population Surveys, Consumer Income, Series P-60.

[4]An alternative to incorporating leisure time into the income concept is to express the needs standard as a function of money and time. See Vickery (1975).

[5]See, for example, the articles by Paglin (1979) and Browning (1975), or a general summary of the argument in Anderson (1979), Chapter 1. The valuation of in-kind benefits is surprisingly difficult. A dollar spent subsidizing rent is not appreciated as much as an extra dollar of income, since the dollar, if given as cash, may have been spent for food, transportation, or something else valued more than the additional housing. Food stamps are the closest in-kind benefit to cash, and if the recipient makes additional food expenditures out of his or her own pocket, then it can be argued that a dollar-for-dollar correspondence exists.

[6]Some analysts have avoided this criticism by treating medical benefits according to their insurance value rather than the full dollar value of benefits actually received.

[7]It may seem unreasonable to expect that a group of some five thousand families can generate accurate estimates for a nation of more than 60 million families. The technical explanation is lengthy, but a simple analogy illustrates the technical principle. In order to test the characteristics of a batch of soup, it is only necessary to take one well-mixed, *representative* spoonful regardless of how large the batch of soup is. The same is true with sample surveys. If the families are chosen carefully to be *representative* of the population of families, then fairly reliable estimates can be made from samples as small as 1,000. Larger samples increase the precision of the estimates (and increase one's ability to make accurate estimates concerning important demographic subgroups of the population), but doubling the size of the sample does not double the precision of the estimate. Furthermore, it takes almost as large a sample to make estimates of the population of a city or state as it does for the nation as a whole.

[8]See Morgan (1977) for a comparison of the characteristics of the Panel Study sample with characteristics of the samples of several large surveys conducted by the Census Bureau.

[9]Minarik (1975) reaches this conclusion after a detailed examination. It may result from the facts that the list of income-related questions is more complete in the Panel Study, the rapport built up through repeated interviewing may make a difference, and respondents may think that a university-based survey organization is less threatening than a governmental one such as the Census Bureau.

[10]The first analyses of the income dynamics of the poor with Panel Study data were presented in Morgan et al. (1974) and Lane and Morgan (1975). Work by Levy (1976) extended this work considerably, as has the work by Coe (1978), Rainwater (1980), and Hill (1981).

[11]An alternative approach would be to compute ten-year *average* income and relate it to ten-year average needs. It has the opposite disadvantage, namely, that one exceptionally good year could cause a family poor in nine of the ten years to have ten-year average

income greater than needs, and thus the family would not be classified as persistently poor. The group of persistently poor (in at least eight of the ten years) is about three-quarters the size of the group with ten-year income less than needs, and there is a great deal of overlapping between them. More than 96 percent of the persistently poor have ten-year average income less than needs, while more than half of the group with ten-year average income less than needs are also persistently poor. Virtually all (97 percent) of the individuals with ten-year income less than needs are poor for at least five of the ten years.

[12]In looking at the entire population over the ten-year period of 1969 through 1978, we must restrict the analysis to those individuals who were living for that entire period. Thus, anyone born after the beginning of 1969 and anyone who died before the end of 1978 was excluded. A similar restriction was imposed on the analysis presented in Table 2.1.

[13]It is tempting to consider all individuals who were poor in only one or two of the ten years as having short spells of poverty. But this would not be entirely accurate, since some who were poor only in 1978 may be in just the beginning of a long spell of poverty that extends beyond 1978, and some who were poor only in 1969 may have been at the end of a long spell that extended prior to 1969. In looking at patterns of poverty in the period from 1970 to 1979, it is found that about 12 percent of the individuals with one or two years of poverty were, in fact, poor in 1979, with about 24 percent more poor in 1970. Indeed, it is possible to cast an analysis of short- and long-run poverty in terms of spells of poverty rather than the incidence of poverty over a specified length of time. Bane and Ellwood (1982) performed such an analysis with data from the Panel Study and found what appeared to be a paradoxical result: of the individuals *coming into contact with poverty*, most turn out to have spells of poverty that last only one or two years; but of all the individuals who are *poor in a given year*, most appeared to be in the midst of a long spell of poverty. The reason for the apparent paradox is that those who do experience long spells simply have a much greater chance of showing up as being poor in a given year.

[14]Similar results were obtained by Rainwater (1980), who developed a relative standard of poverty by ranking all families each year according to their income/needs. The median income/needs was determined by finding the income/needs level that divided the sample of families precisely into two equal groups. The poverty line each year was then defined as one-half of the median income/needs in that year. His poverty line is considerably higher than the official one, so that his estimate of single-year poverty in 1975 (18 percent) was twice as high as the one estimated with the official standard. Confining his analysis to adults age 18 and older, he finds 5.2 percent of the sample was poor by his definition in every one of the ten years between 1967 and 1976, compared with the 2.6 percent figure shown on Table 2.1 based on the official standard. In defining persistent poverty, Rainwater argues that it should include not only those whose incomes fail to rise above his relative poverty line, but should also include those whose incomes are insufficient to escape near-poverty, which he defines as between one-half and seven-tenths of the median income/needs ratio. All in all, 16 percent of the entire adult population are estimated to be in long-term poverty.

[15]The 7.1 percent estimate of poverty in 1978 differs from the 6.8 percent figure shown in Table 2.1 because the two figures are based on slightly different population groups. The 7.1 percent estimate is based on all individuals living during the period from 1974 to 1978. The 6.8 percent estimate is based on the population living during the 1969 to 1978 period and thus excludes children who had not reached the age of five by 1974.

[16]The techniques for analyzing patterns of poverty and other important events are still

in their infancy. Their development has been associated with the growing number of researchers who are analyzing the various longitudinal data sets now available.

[17]The first column of numbers in Table 2.2 is based on all sample individuals who were living in 1978. All other numbers in the table are based on all sample individuals who were living during the entire 1969 to 1978 period.

[18]Since families change composition, this statement can be made more precisely: the 6 percent figure is the fraction of the entire population who lived in families headed by a nonelderly black man *in 1978*. They may have lived in families headed by someone else earlier in the decade. Characteristics that change over time make it difficult to develop a more complete table. For example, rather than fixing the characteristics at a point in time, we could have detailed the poverty fractions according to the number of years the family head was a black man, a woman, etc. Such an analysis was conducted, but did not alter the conclusions based on Table 2.2.

[19]As mentioned above, not all of the group defined as "temporarily poor" experienced short spells of poverty. The problem is that in any given period of years, some individuals will be just beginning or just ending long spells of poverty. Their poverty is temporary in the sense that it did not occur in more than one or two *of the ten years studied*.

[20]Levy's population consists of families headed by nondisabled individuals under the age of 60 whose income exclusive of welfare payments was below the poverty line.

[21]In fact, the definition of "full time" varies somewhat according to the race and sex of household heads but is always within 300 hours of the full-time 2,000 hour mark. In his computations, Levy does not adjust the work hours of household heads with zero work hours—a restriction that applies to less than one-tenth of male household heads and less than one-quarter of female household heads without children. Between one-third and three-fifths of female household heads with children reported zero work hours. Hourly wage rates were calculated by dividing annual labor income by annual work hours.

[22]These averages conceal a great disparity in the *distribution* of unemployment among these household heads. About one-third of the poor household heads escaped unemployment altogether during the nine-year period.

[23]Levy's list of characteristics used to define normal wage rates include: age, education, region, city size, whether disabled, whether union member, and whether a farmer.

[24]Since unemployment rates have been considerably higher in the early 1980's than in the 1960's and 1970's, they may play a more important role in producing poverty. Levy's analysis was conducted for a time period in which the unemployment rate was consistently below 5 percent. However, Corcoran and Hill's (1980) analysis includes the recession of 1974-75 in which the unemployment rate rose to 9 percent.

[25]More specifically, the analysis is restricted to nondisabled male household heads less than age 45 in 1972 whose family income between 1969 and 1971 averaged less than 1.5 times family needs during that period. There were 229 such families. Also included in the analysis were nondisabled female household heads less than 45 years of age in 1972 whose family income in 1971 was less than 1.5 times the official poverty needs standard. There were 257 such families—206 blacks and only 51 whites. The relatively small number of whites precludes a separate analysis for them. The present analysis was undertaken especially for this book, but the general results are similar to those found in Morgan (1974).

[26]As discussed in Chapter 1, this growth rate is calculated from all of the annual observations on family income and family needs during the eight-year period and is adjusted for inflation; accordingly, a positive growth rate indicates that family income/needs

more than kept up with inflation. A growth rate of 9 percent will roughly double a family's income/needs level in this eight-year period.

[27]The initial characteristics included here are identical to those in Chapter 1, except that the initial level of income/needs was included in the predictor list and the index of undue risk avoidance was excluded.

[28]The estimated impact of individual events on income/needs growth rates presented in this section was adjusted statistically for the effects of other events and initial characteristics.

[29]The number of annual work hours used to define labor force status was 500. Individuals reporting more than 500 work hours in a given year were deemed to be in the labor force; those with less than 500 hours were out of the labor force.

[30]Since these regression results have not been published elsewhere, they are detailed in the Appendix to this chapter.

[31]This adjusted race effect was about four-fifths as large as the simple, unadjusted effect.

[32]The achievement motivation measure was administered in the fifth (1972) wave of interviews and was not available for Morgan's 1974 analysis. Other results of interest from the statistical analysis are that an index of connectedness to sources of information and help had a negative effect on income/needs growth, possibly because it captures a propensity to remain fixed geographically and not take advantage of existing opportunities. Income/needs growth was much slower for women in the older age ranges, principally because their chances of remarriage were less favorable.

[33]This program is Title I of the Elementary and Secondary Education Act of 1965 as amended in 1974. Other examples are Title I of the Housing and Community Development Act of 1974 and the Comprehensive Training and Employment Act (CETA) of 1973.

Appendix 2.A

REGRESSION RESULTS ON EFFECTS OF BACKGROUND VARIABLES
ON GROWTH IN INCOME/NEEDS

	Subgroup	
	Initially Poor Male Household Heads	Initially Poor Female Household Heads
Race (whether black)	−.031	−.042*
	(.018)	(.017)
Achievement motivation	.003	.006*
	(.002)	(.003)
Efficacy	.006	.007
	(.003)	(.004)
Future orientation	−.001	−.006
	(.003)	(.004)
Connectedness	.002	−.012**
	(.004)	(.005)
Test score	−.001	.001
	(.003)	(.004)
Education	.005*	.003
	(.002)	(.004)
Age 30 to 34	−.010	−.029
	(.018)	(.026)
Age 35 to 39	.035	−.117**
	(.018)	(.020)
Age 40 to 45	.042*	−.033
	(.019)	(.021)
Initial level	−.064*	−.076**
of income/needs	(.025)	(.020)
R^2 (adjusted)	.086	.255
Standard error of estimate	.09	.12
Number of observations	229	257

*Indicates effect is statistically significant at .05 level.
**Indicates effect is statistically significant at .01 level.

3

The Dynamics of Welfare Use

Several years ago, the *New Yorker* published Susan Sheehan's account of a three-generation welfare family in New York City. Her article, beautifully written, painted a vivid picture of the ways in which the welfare system trapped that family into dependency. Several months after the article's appearance, a professor conducted the following experiment in an undergraduate social science class: he divided the class into three groups, instructing each group to read the article. His instructions to the first group included no other information; but to the second, he explained that the article depicted the experiences of the majority of families that received welfare in this country; he gave the third group the opposite impression, explaining that the article described an atypical welfare family and that the majority of families receiving welfare did so for short periods of time, leading to no intergenerational consequences. Some time after the entire class had read the article, each group was surveyed to see whether they had formed different beliefs about the likelihood of the welfare system to create dependency in its recipients. No differences were found. Despite the divergent information they had been given, all three groups had "bought" the *New Yorker* account as representative.

Case study accounts or personal observations are undoubtedly persuasive. They present a *gestalt*, a far more vivid and complete picture of circumstances than that imparted by statistical studies based on representative samples of families or individuals. An eloquent description of families living in a run-down urban tenement is far more likely to compel our attention than dozens of statistics about the housing characteristics of families who receive welfare income. The obvious danger of case studies, however, is that they may not be representative of any larger group that readers may assume they describe. For example, Sheehan's case study (published in book form in 1976) perpetuates a widespread belief that welfare families are typically headed by women who remain persistently dependent on welfare, and whose children will themselves run a greater risk in adulthood of being dependent upon the welfare system. But available data indicate that this broad stereotype of welfare use is drawn impressionistically from what is actually a small and atypical fraction of welfare recipients.

In this chapter we will investigate the validity of such stereotypes, using information from the Panel Study. As with the incidence of poverty, we find that the receipt of welfare income is surprisingly widespread. Fully one-fourth of the population lived in families that received welfare income in at least one of the ten years between 1969 and 1978. Despite the high incidence of welfare receipt, however, if welfare dependency is defined as counting on welfare income to make up more than one-half of a household's total income, then long-term dependency is rare: less than one-hundredth of the population lived in families that were welfare-dependent for all of the ten years between 1969 and 1978. Thus, while many different families receive welfare income, most do so for fairly short periods of time. And even during the periods when welfare income is received, most receive it as a supplement to income from other sources, principally from work, or they alternate between employment and welfare over the course of a year.

A closer look at families receiving income from welfare sources shows that in as many as half of the cases welfare is used only to bridge a process of digging out following some major crisis—a divorce, a job loss, or perhaps the death of a spouse. The process usually ends with a new foothold in security: a part- or full-time job or, for some female household heads, marriage or remarriage. The remaining half of the welfare cases are roughly split into two very different categories of longer-term dependency: one—about a quarter of all welfare recipients—is made up of those who appear to be using welfare income as part of a more permanent income-packaging strategy; the other quarter is made up of those who appear to be in very serious economic straits, cut off from all other sources of help and very much in need of the resources that welfare provides.

Studies of the intergenerational dynamics of welfare use, drawing on Panel Study data, provide mixed evidence on the contention that welfare receipt is passed on from one generation to another. Among women who have left the homes of parents who received welfare income, most are *not* likely to be receiving welfare themselves. But when these women are compared with otherwise similar women whose parents did not receive welfare income, those from welfare recipient backgrounds show a somewhat greater likelihood to be receiving welfare. In general, the parents' overall economic status is a more powerful determinant of subsequent welfare use by adult children than is the parents' welfare status itself.

Another important question raised by the present welfare system is whether it has the unintended side effects of encouraging divorce and separation, discouraging remarriage, or encouraging illegitimate births. The evidence from the Panel Study indicates few, if any, effects of this kind.

Throughout the empirical sections of this chapter, "welfare income" includes payments to a husband and wife (or to a single head of the household) from most of the major noncontributory cash transfer programs as well as the dollar value of benefits from one of the major in-kind benefit programs: food stamps.[1] This set of welfare programs includes:

1. *Aid to Families with Dependent Children (AFDC)*. Designed to provide assistance to female heads and, in some states, to male heads of families with dependent children, total expenditures for this program in 1978 were $10.7 billion.[2]

2. *Supplemental Security Income (SSI)*. Begun in 1974 as a consolidation of several programs to help the aged, blind, and disabled, SSI program expenditures amounted to $6.6 billion in 1978.

3. *"Other welfare."* Included in this category is income from all noncontributory transfer programs other than AFDC and SSI, as reported by Panel Study respondents. Much of what is reported here is income from state-administered General Assistance payments, but it also includes the various programs that were consolidated to form the SSI program in 1974.

4. *Food Stamps*. Strictly speaking, the food stamp program is not a cash welfare program, but it will be included along with the cash programs in this chapter. Until 1979, food stamps were allotted in amounts representing food costs based on family size, and were purchased at a cost determined by family income. The difference between a family's

food stamp allotment and the purchase price paid by the family was the bonus value of the food stamps—the amount used in this chapter to measure food stamp benefits.[3] Since 1979, the purchase price requirement has been eliminated. The cost of the food stamp program in 1978 was $5.2 billion.

Several other major in-kind welfare programs are not included in the present empirical work. The largest of these is Medicaid ($17.8 billion in 1978), followed by the $3.7 billion (in 1978) housing assistance program and the $3.4 billion child nutrition program.

Incidence of Welfare Program Participation

Although growth in the cost and coverage of the various programs constituting the welfare system is easy to document, the dynamics of individual involvement are not. The basic problem is similar to that of understanding the dynamics of poverty. Yearly information on the extent of poverty reveals next to nothing about the extent to which the same individuals are poor from one year to the next. Similarly, annual counts of beneficiaries of the various welfare programs tell us little about either the dynamics of an individual's involvement with welfare or the proportion of the total population affected in some way by at least one of the programs.

Little attention has been paid to studies of several individual welfare programs that indicate considerable turnover in the recipient population. In a study of case records of the AFDC program in New York City, Rydell et al. (1974) found that only about one-quarter of those receiving AFDC benefits between 1967 and 1972 could be classified as long-term recipients and that half of the cases were on the rolls for one year or less. An examination of California AFDC case records by Boskin and Nold (1975) showed slightly less turnover than found by the Rydell study, but still much more than is commonly believed. Using the national representative data on AFDC recipients from the Panel Study, Rein and Rainwater (1978) found that of the women who received income from the AFDC program during the period from 1967 to 1973, less than one-sixth received such assistance for all seven of the years under study, and a much smaller proportion relied on it to make up more than half of their total family income for all seven years.

This high degree of turnover shows up in the food stamp program as well. Coe (1981) used Panel Study information to study food stamp program participation, and found that over the four-year period between

Table 3.1
INCIDENCE OF SHORT- AND LONG-RUN WELFARE RECEIPT AND DEPENDENCE,
1969–1978

	Percent U.S. Population:	
	Receiving Any Welfare Income	Dependent on Welfare for More than 50% of Family Income
Welfare in 1978	8.1%	3.5%
Welfare in 1 or more years, 1969–78	25.2	8.7
Welfare in 5 or more years, 1969–78	8.3	3.5
Welfare in all 10 years, 1969–78	2.0	0.7
"Persistent welfare" (welfare in 8 or more years, 1969–78)	4.4	2.0

Note: "Welfare" is defined as AFDC, General Assistance and other welfare, Supplemental Security Income, and food stamps received by the head of household or wife. "Welfare Dependence" is defined as welfare income received by the head or wife amounting to more than half of their combined incomes.
Table reads: "In 1978, 8.1% of the U.S. population lived in families that received some welfare income."

1973 and 1976 only one fifth of the families participating in the food stamp program did so every one of the four years.

Panel Study information provides a national scope and a ten-year time span for an analysis of patterns of welfare use. Two kinds of beneficiaries are distinguished: first, "welfare recipients," those living in families where the head or wife received at least one dollar of cash income or food stamp bonus income from any of these welfare programs; and second, "welfare dependents," for whom welfare income going to the head or wife amounted to at least half of the total income of the head and wife.[4]

Table 3.1 shows the incidence of welfare receipt and welfare dependence for the population as a whole. Although the receipt of welfare income is quite pervasive, it is not nearly as persistent as many would believe. More than one-quarter of the United States population is estimated to have lived in families where some form of welfare income was received in at least one year between 1969 and 1978. Food stamps were the only form of welfare for many of these families; excluding them, the fraction receiving welfare income at least once drops from one-quarter to about one-sixth. The incidence of welfare receipt is not uniform across different segments of our society. While 25 percent of the entire population received income from welfare sources in at least one of the ten years, the comparable figure for all blacks was 67 percent, and for black children (under the age of ten in 1969) it was an astonishing 73 percent.

Turnover in the welfare rolls is evidenced by the much smaller proportions of the population receiving income from welfare sources for several of the ten years. Less than 10 percent of the population received welfare income for at least five of the ten years, and only 2 percent received it for all ten years. If we define "persistent" welfare recipients in accordance with the definition of persistent poverty in the last chapter, we find that only about one-sixth of the group that ever received welfare were persistent welfare recipients (for at least eight of the ten years).

Families rarely rely exclusively on welfare income; instead, welfare appears to be used to supplement income from labor market earnings and other sources or as an alternative source of income when other sources dry up.[5] Since "welfare dependency" implies a family that is relying heavily on welfare income, it is useful to define dependency by drawing a line at half of all income received by the head or wife and then calculating the fraction of the population living in families where welfare income received by the head amounted to more than that fraction.[6] The second column of figures in Table 3.1 show that for any of the periods selected, less than half of those who received welfare income were dependent on it for more than half of their annual income. So, while 25 percent of the population lived in families where some welfare income was received in at least one of the ten years between 1969 and 1978, less than 9 percent of the population was dependent upon it for at least one of these years. Longer-term dependency is even less frequent: less than 4 percent of the population was dependent upon welfare income for at least five of the ten years, and less than 1 percent was dependent for all ten years.

The incidence of welfare receipt and dependence is summarized in Figure 3.1. Most of the population (74.8 percent) received no welfare income during the ten years between 1969 and 1978. Of the 25.2 percent who did, about half received welfare for only one or two of the ten years. Persistent welfare recipients make up about 17 percent of those receiving any welfare income, and between 4 and 5 percent of the entire population. But fewer than half of these persistent *recipients* were also persistently *dependent*, relying on welfare to make up more than half of

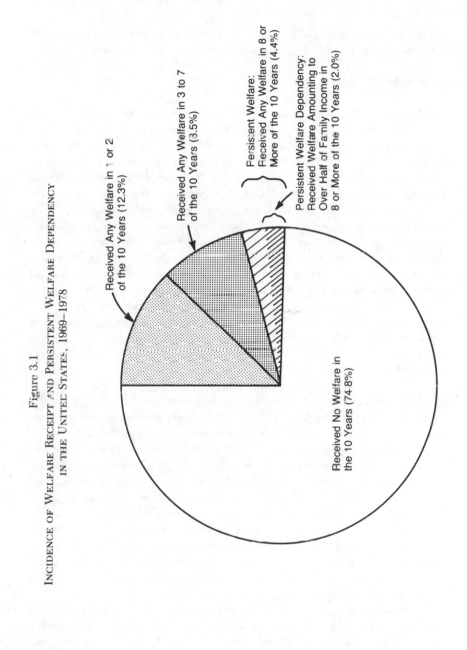

Figure 3.1

INCIDENCE OF WELFARE RECEIPT AND PERSISTENT WELFARE DEPENDENCY
IN THE UNITED STATES, 1969–1978

their family income. Thus in all, only 2 percent of the population could be classified as persistently dependent upon welfare income.

Combining Welfare and Work

The fact that many families receiving welfare payments do not rely exclusively on welfare runs contrary to popular stereotypes. In a study covering seven years (1967-1973) of Panel Study information, Rein and Rainwater (1978) took a closer look at the ways in which families combine welfare income and income from other sources into a total family income "package," and found that jobs provided the main nonwelfare sources of income for families not relying exclusively on welfare.[7] For women periodically on and off welfare, earned income was more important than welfare income, and for all but the small number who were heavily dependent on welfare, earnings averaged more than half the amount of welfare income. Other income sources—alimony and child support payments and various other public and private transfers—were less important. During the years that the intermittent welfare recipients were not receiving welfare benefits, their income "packages" resembled those of comparable families that never received welfare.

Patterns of Welfare Use

The transient contact of many families with welfare should not be taken as evidence that the patterns of welfare receipt are utterly random. Rein and Rainwater (1978) examined these patterns for adult women during the period from 1967 to 1973 and found evidence that the chances of staying on welfare for an additional year increased with each year of welfare receipt. Of adult women (regardless of marital status) who had received no welfare income in a given year, only one in sixty-five received it the following year. Of all women who began to receive welfare in a given year, about three in five continued to receive it the subsequent year. Of women with two consecutive years on welfare, an even higher proportion, seven in ten, received it the subsequent year, and this proportion increased to about eight in ten for women who had been on welfare for four consecutive years.

Evidence also indicates that women who have just recently gone off welfare are more likely to start again than are those who had been off for several years. About one in four of the women who quit in a given year started up again in the next. Once a woman had been off for several years, her chances of receiving welfare fell to about one in fifteen. These figures should not be taken as proof that prior welfare receipt *causes* subsequent welfare dependency, however. As with the poverty patterns discussed in Chapter 2, it is difficult to isolate the effects of welfare itself from the characteristics and circumstances of those who receive it.

Characteristics of Welfare Recipients

Just as with poverty, high turnover among welfare recipients raises the possibility that a snapshot picture of welfare recipients afforded by cross-section data may provide a distorted view of the characteristics of temporary and persistent welfare recipients. We found persistent poverty more heavily concentrated among blacks, female-headed households, and families living in the South than is indicated by one-year figures. A parallel look at long-term welfare recipients, shown in Table 3.2, reveals a similar profile with the exception that persistent welfare recipients tended to be concentrated in urban areas.

The structure of Table 3.2 is similar to Table 2.2 in Chapter 2. Each entry shows the composition of a particular subgroup, as described by the column headings. The first entry reveals that 57 percent of all individuals living in families where either the head or wife received welfare income in 1978 were in female-headed households.[8] The next two entries in that row show that female-headed families were overrepresented (67 percent) among persistent welfare recipients, and constituted an even larger share (78 percent) of the smaller group that was persistently dependent on welfare sources for more than half of all income received by the head or wife. In contrast, the fraction of temporary welfare recipients living in female-headed families (19 percent) is identical to the fraction of individuals living in those families in the population as a whole.

As with the comparable data on poverty in Chapter 2 (Table 2.2), Table 3.2 shows striking similarities between the characteristics of temporary welfare recipients and the population as a whole. Welfare recipients in 1978, as might be expected, were overrepresented among female-headed families—particularly those headed by black women—and among individuals living in families headed by a disabled individual. The overrepresentation is greater for both persistent welfare receipt and persistent welfare dependence than for one-year welfare receipt. Nearly four-fifths of those persistently dependent on welfare lived in families headed by a woman, and, while one-year welfare recipients living in

Table 3.2

DEMOGRAPHIC CHARACTERISTICS OF ONE-YEAR WELFARE RECIPIENTS, PERSISTENT WELFARE RECIPIENTS, PERSISTENT WELFARE DEPENDENTS, AND TEMPORARY WELFARE RECIPIENTS, 1969–1978

Characteristics of 1978 Household Head	Welfare Recipient in 1978	Persistent Recipients		Temporary Recipients	
		Received Any Welfare 8 or more Years, 1969–78	Dependent on Welfare in 8 or more Years, 1969–78	Received Welfare in 1 or 2 Years, 1969–78	Entire U.S. Population
All Females	57%	67%	78%	19%	19%
Elderly	9	10	7	4	5
Nonelderly					
White	24	21	27	10	10
Black	24	37	44	4	4
All Males	43	33	21	81	81
Elderly	6	7	0	6	8
Nonelderly					
White	29	15	16	66	66
Black	8	11	5	9	7
Rural (town of 10,000 or less)	15	13	7	15	15
Urban (city of 500,000 or more)	34	44	55	31	32
Southern U.S.	34	34	28	38	30
Disabled	29	42	33	14	10
Black	38	55	52	15	12
Number of observations	2,709	1,426	700	1,771	15,753
Estimated fraction of entire population in group	8.1%	4.4%	2.0%	12.3%	100.0%

Note: "Welfare" is defined as AFDC, General Assistance and other welfare, Supplemental Security Income, and food stamps received by the head of household or wife. "Welfare dependence" is defined as welfare income received by the head of household or wife amounting to more than half of their combined income.

Table reads: "Of all individuals receiving welfare income in 1978, 57% lived in families headed by a woman. Of the entire U.S. population, only 19% lived in families headed by a woman."

female-headed families were equally divided by race, persistent welfare receipt and dependence were more likely for families headed by black women than for those headed by white women. Nevertheless, fewer than half of the individuals found to be persistently dependent on welfare lived in families headed by a nonelderly black woman in 1978.

In the previous chapter substantial differences were noted in the geographic distribution of the persistent versus the one-year poor. The figures for one-year welfare recipients indicate that their location was quite similar to the population as a whole—nearly equal proportions of both groups lived in large urban areas, in rural areas, or in the South. Persistent welfare recipients, on the other hand, were much more likely to be living in large urban areas. Only about one-third of all 1978 welfare recipients lived in cities of 500,000 or more, whereas more than half of those persistently dependent on welfare income lived in cities of that size.

The characteristics of short- and longer-term welfare recipients are indicative of the processes that lead families to go on welfare. Coe (1981) took a more detailed look at this by pooling Panel Study information for the ten-year period between 1969 and 1978.[9] He found that the chances of beginning to receive welfare income were heavily influenced by family composition changes and untoward labor market events. A divorce or separation increased the chances that an adult woman would begin to receive welfare by about ten percentage points but did not increase the likelihood that a man would go on welfare. The birth of children also increased these chances for families headed by women and blacks, as did the continued presence of young children in the household. Adverse employment factors—a high rate of unemployment in the county of residence, or involuntary job loss or extensive unemployment of the household head, for any reason—all significantly increased a family's chances of beginning to receive income from welfare sources. All told, however, the family composition variables were the strongest predictors of whether or not a family began to receive welfare income.

A Qualitative Look at Welfare Recipients

In an attempt to understand the dynamics of the welfare system, Anderson-Khleif (1976) performed a detailed analysis of 92 randomly selected Panel Study female-headed families with some welfare experience. She found that they fell into three broad groups: (1) a transition group using welfare to cope with an economic crisis caused by the death, disability, or departure of a husband; (2) a group "locked into" the welfare system with little prospect of improvement; and (3) a group using welfare income along with other income sources that rarely included earnings from work.

Roughly half of the women surveyed were in the transition group. The vast majority of women who had children and were going through a divorce did not rely on the welfare system for support. However, among those who did, reliance on welfare was heavy before their children were old enough to go to school but decreased afterwards, with the increasing chances that the women might find a part-time or full-time job or remarry.

The rest of the women were evenly divided into the two other groups, exhibiting two very different kinds of dependence on welfare income sources. One, quite cut off from other sources of help and support, appeared to be in serious trouble, with little chance for self-improvement. The other group was firmly connected into the various government-assistance programs available for families with children, and also had friends or relatives living nearby from whom support could be drawn.

Intergenerational Aspects of Welfare Use

A particular concern about welfare programs is that they may lead succeeding generations into welfare dependency. But while there are instances in which children from welfare families go on welfare themselves once they split off and form their own households, it is crucial to ascertain whether these are isolated instances or the norm. Panel Study data make it possible to investigate this question, since the procedures used provide for interviews with adults who entered the study as children in their parental households and subsequently left home to form their own families. Earlier interviews with their parents reveal whether they received welfare income, and later interviews with the young "split-off" children provide corresponding information for them. Although the existing data on the receipt of welfare by children cover only the few years after they leave home, these data appear to be the best source of information available to address this question.

Levy (1980) has taken the most thorough look at the intergenerational aspects of welfare by examining Panel Study women who split off from their parental homes between 1968 and 1976. He found that about 3 percent of these women were unmarried heads of their own families with children and receiving welfare income in 1976, and that women who came from families that were receiving welfare in 1968 were 1.4 times more likely to be in this group of welfare recipients in 1976. To illustrate this effect, Levy compares probable outcomes for several scenarios. One takes the case of a woman whose characteristics were average in most respects[10] except that her parental family in 1968 was headed by a woman, had family income just at the poverty line, and did *not* receive income from welfare. Of the white women in this situation, about 7 percent received welfare income in 1976, while of the black women, about 25 percent received welfare in 1976. In the second scenario, the only change is that the family *had* received income from welfare sources. In this case, the fraction receiving welfare in 1976 increased to 11 percent for white women and about 36 percent for black women.

While this effect is sizable, nonetheless most women coming from welfare families were *not* receiving welfare in 1976. Moreover, the welfare status of parents was a much less important factor in determining the welfare status of their children than was the parents' income level. A final qualification is that Levy's analysis was of welfare receipt in a single year rather than of long-term dependency. We found earlier that fewer than one-quarter of those receiving welfare in a given year were persistently dependent upon it.[11]

Effects of Welfare on Family Composition

The Aid to Families with Dependent Children (AFDC) program generally restricts its benefits to families with female heads and children.[12] Many fear that these restrictions may have the unintended consequences of encouraging divorce, discouraging marriage or remarriage, and possibly encouraging illegitimate births. Given the important role played by family composition changes on changes in economic status, the issue of the effects of welfare on family composition is clearly an important one.

As pointed out by Lane (1981) in his review of evidence from the Panel Study on this issue, research on the possible effects of AFDC is hindered by the fact that it is not possible to compare the behavior of individuals in the current AFDC system with that of individuals living in a comparable world that offers no AFDC system, simply because the latter does not exist.[13] Instead, the strategy must be to compare individuals living in states with relatively large benefits to "otherwise similar" individuals living in states with smaller benefits. The "otherwise similar" condition is produced by an analysis that adjusts statistically for the other factors that may affect divorce, remarriage, or births.

A number of studies have looked for these possible effects of AFDC, each of them differing somewhat in the years of data used, the composition of the sample chosen, and the variables used in the statistical analysis. Lane concludes that "findings of this research have *not* shown convincingly that the availability of *more* rather than *some* AFDC makes much if any difference in rates of divorce–separation, remarriage, or illegitimacy" (Lane, 1981, p.37; emphasis in original). It was not the case that every study conducted with Panel Study data failed to find effects. But either the effects that were found were not quantitatively large or similar studies failed to replicate the results. Further research is clearly needed in this area, but the work done thus far supports the tentative conclusion that there are no major effects of AFDC on family composition decisions.

The "Decision" Not to Participate

Most welfare benefits are geared to the level of family income, and thus people's decisions regarding welfare benefits may involve decisions about other sources of income, most notably from employment. Large-scale experiments have been conducted to measure the possible work disincentives of welfare programs. The Panel Study has little evidence to add on this matter, although it does provide valuable information on a different and often overlooked question: Why do individuals who are eligible for welfare benefits "choose" not to partake of them?

It is popularly assumed that nearly all persons who are eligible to participate in welfare programs do so. In *Welfare*, Anderson writes "(t)here will be isolated instances where a person is unaware of being eligible, or is unjustly denied aid by a welfare bureaucrat, or simply chooses not to accept the social stigma of being on welfare. But these cases are the exceptions" (Anderson, 1978, pp. 37-38). Although the proportion of eligibles who participate in the AFDC program is quite high, participation rates for several other welfare programs are not. Several studies have estimated that fewer than half of the households eligible to participate in the food stamp program in fact do so.[14] The participation rate of eligible elderly in the SSI program has been placed at around 55 percent (Warlick, 1982). Why are these rates so low?

Economic explanations of participation decisions focus on comparisons of the level of program benefits with the costs of participation. "Costs" may be defined broadly to include transportation and other access costs, as well as the psychological costs of dealing with the welfare bureaucracy or with the stigma attached to recipients.

To investigate the relative importance of these factors for participation in the food stamp program, nonparticipating Panel Study respondents were asked in 1976 whether they thought they were eligible for food stamp benefits and, if so, why they didn't take advantage of such benefits. An analysis of responses by Coe (1979) found that 60 percent of eligible nonparticipants did not think or did not know that they were eligible to receive food stamps. No other reason—such as low bonus value, administrative hassle, or attitudes—was given in as much as 10 percent of the responses. Poor information was found to be particularly important in explaining the low participation rates of the elderly, the employed, the childless, and those who were not participating in other welfare programs. Thus "choices" regarding whether or not to participate in welfare programs may be dominated by misinformation.

Effect of Welfare Income on the Incidence of Poverty

By the late 1970s, much had been written about our victory in the war on poverty. Anderson (1978) made the most unqualified proclamation of victory: "The 'war on poverty' that began in 1964 has been won. The growth of jobs and income in the private economy, combined with an explosive increase in government spending for welfare and income transfer programs, has virtually eliminated poverty in the United States. Any Americans who truly cannot care for themselves are now eligible for generous government aid in the form of cash, medical benefits, food stamps, housing, and other services" (Anderson, 1978, p.15).

In this section, we examine the effects of welfare programs on short- and longer-term poverty. Our estimates include cash program benefits received by family heads and wives as well as the benefits from a major in-kind program, food stamps. Since benefits from some other important in-kind welfare programs have not been measured, we cannot give a definitive estimate of the distribution of all government welfare benefits to low-income families.

The effects of cash welfare programs on the incidence of short- and long-run poverty are shown in Table 3.3. The first column repeats the relevant figures discussed in Chapter 2. The second shows the extent of poverty if cash welfare payments received by the head and wife are

Table 3.3

EFFECT OF CASH WELFARE PROGRAMS ON THE INCIDENCE OF SHORT- AND
LONG-RUN POVERTY, 1969–1978

	Percent of U.S. Population Poor if Poverty Defined As:	
	Total Money Income Less than Needs (Official Definition)	Total Money Income —Excluding Cash Welfare Less than Needs
Poor in 1978	6.8%	8.3%
Poor in 1 or more years, 1969–78	24.4	25.8
Poor in 5 or more years, 1969–78	5.4	8.5
Poor in all 10 years, 1969–78	0.7	1.7
"Persistently poor": (poor in 8 or more years, 1969–78)	2.6	4.4

Note: "Cash welfare" is defined as AFDC, General Assistance and other welfare, and
Supplemental Security Income received by the head of household or wife.
Table reads: "6.8% of the U.S. population was poor in 1978, according to the official
definition of poverty. If cash welfare income is subtracted from total family income, the
proportion of the population found to be poor increases to 8.3%."

excluded from family income. The comparison indicates that cash welfare income is targeted toward society's most needy members: it has a
substantial effect on the incidence of persistent poverty but virtually no
effect on temporary poverty.

Beginning with the one-year figures, Table 3.3 shows that one-year
poverty would have increased by one-fifth (from 6.8 percent to 8.3
percent of the entire population) if the cash welfare payments had not
been received.[15] Since the group of individuals poor in any one year will
consist of some who are only temporarily poor as well as those who are
persistently poor, it is important to determine whether welfare payments are well targeted towards the persistently poor. Those figures
show that this is indeed the case. Without welfare income, the incidence
of persistent poverty would have been 69 percent higher (4.4 percent
versus 2.6 percent of the population). In contrast, the fraction of the
population that had at least occasional contact with poverty rose only
slightly, from 24.4 percent to 25.8 percent.

The food stamp program has become a major source of assistance to
low-income families. Since its benefits are not received in the form of
cash, however, it has no effect on the official count of the nation's poor.

Table 3.4

EFFECTS OF ADDING FOOD STAMP "INCOME" ON THE INCIDENCE OF SHORT-
AND LONG-RUN POVERTY, 1974–1978

	Percent of U.S. Population Poor if Poverty Defined As:	
	Total Family Income Less than Needs (Official Definition)	Total Family Income Plus Bonus Value of Food Stamps is Less than Needs
Poor in 1978	7.1%	6.4%
Poor in 1 or more years, 1974–78	16.6	15.3
Poor in all 5 years, 1974–78	1.8	1.3

Table reads: "7.1% of the U.S. population was poor in 1978, using the official definition of poverty. The addition of the bonus value of food stamps to total family income reduces the estimated incidence of poverty to 6.4%."

Table 3.4 shows how the addition to family income of the bonus value of food stamps received by the head of household or wife changes the estimated incidence of short- and long-run poverty. Since the program did not reach its present dimensions until 1974, it would be difficult to assess its impact accurately over the entire ten-year period prior to 1978. Accordingly, Table 3.4 is limited to showing the effects on the incidence of poverty during the five-year period between 1974 and 1978.

The food stamp program was successful in lifting some families out of poverty. In 1978 the proportion who were poor fell by about one-tenth (from 7.1 percent to 6.4 percent) when food stamp income was included.[16] The resulting decrease in the estimated number of individuals in poverty was about half as large as the estimated decrease brought about by the receipt of welfare income.

Like welfare income, food stamps also reduced the incidence of persistent poverty, but these effects were not as large as those of welfare income, nor as effectively targeted away from those only temporarily poor. The incidence of five-year poverty declined from 1.8 percent to 1.3 percent; the incidence of poverty in one of the five years declined from 16.6 percent to 15.3 percent. However, providing food stamps for the temporarily poor may be as desirable as providing for the persistently poor, since the food stamp program is intended to fill short-term food needs as well as longer-term nutrition and health needs.

Table 3.5

INCIDENCE OF WELFARE RECEIPT AMONG THE PREWELFARE NONPOOR,
TEMPORARILY POOR, AND PERSISTENTLY POOR, 1969–1978

	Percent Receiving Cash Welfare or Food Stamps In:	
	1 or More Years	5 or More Years
Nonpoor	11.7%	0.5%
"Temporarily poor" (poor, excluding welfare income, in only 1 or 2 years, 1969–78)	41.7	4.6
"Intermittently poor" (poor, excluding welfare income, in 3–7 years, 1969–78)	78.9	42.7
"Persistently poor" (poor, excluding welfare income, in 8 or more years, 1969–78)	96.9	84.2

Note: "Welfare" is defined as AFDC, General Assistance and other welfare, Supplemental Security Income, and food stamps received by the head or wife.
Table reads: "11.7% of individuals living in families whose incomes, excluding welfare benefits, were above the poverty line in all ten years received welfare benefits at least once. Only 0.5% of them received welfare benefits in at least five of the ten years."

Incidence of Welfare Receipt among Poor Families

We have seen that welfare income lifts some families above the poverty line and that its benefits are relatively greater for the persistently poor than for the temporarily poor. The low participation rates in some welfare programs, however, raise the possibility that some of those most persistently in need of assistance are not receiving it. It becomes important, then, to look at the incidence of welfare receipt among individuals with different types of experience with poverty, as described in Table 3.5. All sample individuals were classified according to their economic experience during the decade between 1969 and 1978. Poverty is defined by comparing the poverty level needs standard with total family income excluding welfare income received by the head and wife.[17] All individuals were classified according to whether prewelfare income during the decade was always *greater* than needs ("nonpoor"), or whether prewelfare income was *below* needs in one or two years (temporarily poor), three to seven years (intermittently poor), or eight to ten (all) years (persistently poor). For each of these groups, the fractions in which the head or wife received cash welfare or food stamps at least once during the ten years and in five or more of the ten years are distinguished.

In general, Table 3.5 shows extensive coverage by the welfare system for the most needy, and modest coverage for other individuals. Of individuals who would have been persistently poor in the absence of welfare income, almost 97 percent received some welfare benefits, and more than 84 percent received benefits in at least five of the ten years.[18] Although the adequacy of the benefits can be questioned (recall from Table 3.4 that more than half of these persistently poor remained so after cash welfare benefits were added to family income), Table 3.5 shows that virtually none of these individuals were completely cut off from aid.

As might be expected, coverage for the intermittently and temporarily poor was considerably less. Nearly four-fifths of the former group received welfare benefits at least once, compared with about two-fifths of the latter group. Very few (4.6 percent) of those found to be temporarily poor received such benefits more than half the time. More than one-tenth of the individuals who were above the poverty line in all ten years received income from welfare sources at least once; virtually none of them received benefits for more than half of those years.

Summary and Implications

Welfare should provide assistance to those in need, assure an adequate standard of living, and encourage all who need assistance to seek it; but should not lead those confronting only temporary hardship to develop longer-term dependency. The potential conflict in these goals is self-evident.[19]

As demonstrated in the last chapter, the extent of economic need differs among people. A surprisingly large number of persons face difficult economic circumstances at one time or another; one-quarter of the population was poor at least once during the 1970s. For most, the adversity is temporary, but for some, it is more persistent, with little prospect of improvement. So at any given time, the welfare system must provide for both the temporarily and the permanently needy. It must provide adequate support and simultaneously offer incentives to leave the system. How well does our present welfare system meet these conflicting goals?

A first bit of evidence from the Panel Study is that the welfare system touches a surprisingly large fraction of our society. One out of every four Americans lived in a household that received income from one of the major welfare programs at least once over a ten-year period. The record of coverage for individual welfare programs is far from perfect—only half of the eligible households in a given year participate in the food stamp program and in the Supplemental Security Income program for the elderly. Participation rates in the AFDC program, on the other hand, are generally thought to be considerably higher. But taken together, Panel Study information indicates that the welfare system delivered at least some assistance to nearly 50 percent of the temporarily poor and to over 95 percent of the persistently poor. Barriers to the welfare system exist, but apparently they are not so formidable as to prevent a substantial segment of the population from receiving assistance in time of need.

The fact that over a ten-year period the number of people who receive any welfare is considerably larger than over a one-year span indicates that the current system does not foster large-scale dependency. One-half of the persons who lived in families where welfare benefits were received at least once in a decade did not receive it in more than two of the ten years. Thus the greater share of welfare recipients clearly did not come to rely on welfare as a long-term means of support. These temporary recipients represent a cross section of the American population. No broad demographic group in our society appears immune from shocks to their usual standard of living, shocks resulting from rapidly changing economic or personal conditions. For men, the shock often comes in the form of an involuntary job loss; for married women, divorce or the death of the spouse is often the precipitating event. Such events may not always be totally unavoidable, but few people are immune to occasional economic misfortune, and when it strikes, welfare serves as a kind of insurance for them, providing temporary assistance until they are able to regain their more customary levels of living. In the words of Rein and Rainwater, these people are "digging out" following a disaster. Welfare assists during that process and then, in time, is left behind.

That the welfare system does not foster extensive dependency is also reflected in the fact that, even in the year they receive it, most welfare recipients are not *dependent* on welfare income. Although one out of four Americans were in households that received welfare at some time in a ten-year period, fewer than one in ten was ever in a household in which more than half of the annual income of the head and wife came from welfare sources. Since much of the other income comes from work, work and welfare appear to go together in most cases. Furthermore, even among those people who were dependent on welfare at some time, nearly half were dependent in only one or two years of the ten-year period. Eventually they find other sources of income, in amounts sufficient to enable them either to leave the welfare rolls altogether or at least to greatly reduce their reliance on welfare income. Thus *dependency* is the exception rather than the rule among welfare recipients, and only about 2 percent of the entire population could be characterized as *persistently* dependent upon welfare income during the late 1960s and 1970s.

A related issue of dependency is the extent to which it is transmitted from one generation to another. Conventional wisdom holds that a child growing up in a welfare household will become accustomed to a life on welfare and will, in adulthood, also go on welfare, thus perpetuating a syndrome of dependency. But the underlying premise of long-term dependency implied by this view is contradicted by the fact that most welfare recipients are not dependent on welfare and that most of the remainder are dependent only for short periods. The issue of intergenerational transmission of welfare dependency is even more directly addressed by evidence showing that most adult children from welfare families were not receiving welfare income themselves, and most of the adults who were receiving welfare income did not come from welfare households.

A more subtle policy question is whether the receipt of welfare income by parents increases the chances of a child receiving it. The evidence from several different investigations provides no clear answer, but even when some intergenerational effects can be found, the mechanism by which they operate is unclear. Is it because of attitudes and values (as conventional wisdom would have it) or is it merely because the earlier family experience provides better information about the availability and the rules of welfare programs? The evidence is that low participation rates among those eligible for the food stamp program are largely caused by a lack of information about eligibility. This suggests that information may play a role in the intergenerational process as well.

In sum, then, it is clear that most welfare recipients remain on the welfare rolls for relatively short periods of time; that most are never dependent on welfare income in a given year; and that, even for those who are, this dependency is short-lived. But this rather optimistic appraisal of the welfare system must be tempered by the fact that there is a group of people who remain on the welfare rolls more or less permanently, and a subgroup that is permanently dependent on welfare income for their support. Neither group is large: of all who had ever received welfare, only 17 percent received it in at least eight of the ten years studied and only 8 percent of all recipients were dependent on welfare income for at least eight years. Both of these smaller groups are distinct from the population as a whole; they are disproportionately female, black, and have children in the home. It should come as no surprise that these are also the groups most susceptible to persistent poverty. As argued in Chapter 2, it is difficult to see options other than welfare for many in this group, who are faced with the prospect of low wages and burdened with child-care responsibilities. Their reliance on direct public transfers may be a necessity.

But perhaps there is some hope. Fewer than half of the long-term welfare recipients are permanently dependent on welfare, indicating that the possibility of earning other income may still be a viable option, even if welfare income is necessary to provide the basic necessities. For this group, the welfare system should perhaps focus less on how to remove them from the welfare rolls altogether and more on how to alter the mix of welfare and other income while maintaining an adequate level of living. Evidence that welfare transitions for women are affected by changes in their wages suggests that a program of wage subsidies might be effective in promoting more labor market activity.

It was noted at the outset that a fundamental dilemma of the welfare system was how to provide adequate support for the needy and still encourage a return to self-sufficiency among those who are able to do so. The broad picture outlined here indicates that the system has been successful in avoiding long-term dependency. But we also found evidence that while welfare income can provide a cushion against temporary economic hardships, the benefit levels do not provide enough support to lift households out of temporary poverty. While the effect of welfare income on the incidence of persistent poverty is more dramatic, more than half of the individuals who would have been persistently poor without welfare income would still remain poor after such benefits are added in. Although the benefits have softened the economic hardship faced by recipient households, they have not been sufficient to provide even the official poverty line's austere standard of living. Seen in this light, the question remains whether we can design a welfare system with benefit levels high enough to eliminate poverty, especially persistent poverty, while simultaneously ensuring that long-term dependency is not encouraged.

Notes

[1]Excluded are *contributory* transfer programs, for which individuals and their employers may contribute money that entitles them to receive payments under certain circumstances. The largest such programs are Social Security, workers' compensation, and unemployment compensation.

[2]Expenditure figures in this section are from the U.S. Bureau of the Census (1980).

[3]Because food stamp information was not gathered in 1973, the bonus value of the stamps for that year cannot be added to other welfare income.

[4]More natural definitions of welfare receipt and welfare dependency would be, respectively, (1) if *any* family member receives income from welfare sources; and (2) if the combined welfare payments of family members amounts to more than half of the *total* family income. Panel Study information on the transfer income received by individuals in the family other than the head or wife is not detailed enough for the years prior to 1974 to permit these definitions. An analysis of the five-year period between 1974 and 1978 showed that the picture of welfare receipt and dependency from income information for the head and wife only is very similar to the situation based on figures on income from all family members. For example, 19.1 percent of the population were estimated to be living in families where welfare income was received by the head or wife in at least one of the five years between 1974 and 1978, and 4.5 percent lived in families where the head or wife received welfare income all five years. The estimated fractions living in families where *any* member of the family received welfare income at least one or all five years were 21.6 and 4.7 percent, respectively. The estimated incidence of welfare dependency actually decreases when the definition of dependency is changed from a situation in which welfare income of the head and wife makes up more than one-half of the total income of the head and wife to a situation where all welfare income makes up more than half of the total family income. Estimated dependency in at least one year out of the five falls from 6.6 percent to 5.9 percent. Estimated dependency in every one of the five years falls from 1.9 to 1.1 percent.

[5]The Panel Study data on incomes are for entire calendar years, and we cannot distinguish families who receive two types of income simultaneously from those who alternate between sources over the course of a year.

[6]The bonus value of food stamps received by the head or wife is included in both the numerator and denominator of this dependency ratio.

[7]See also the work of Harrison (1977), based on Panel Study information.

[8]In Table 3.2, an individual is counted as a welfare recipient if the head or wife of the family in which he or she lives received income from welfare sources (including food stamps). The table presents information spanning ten years, so only individuals who were ten years of age or older in 1978 were included in each of the computations. A similar sample restriction produced the figures for 1978.

[9]Hutchens (1981) also conducted a detailed investigation of entry into and exit from the AFDC program between 1970 and 1971 for families with female heads who remained unmarried. He focused on the effects of AFDC program parameters and wage rates on participation. Entry and exit decisions were affected by the level of benefits for those with no labor income and by changes in wage rates reported by the female heads, but not by the extent to which program benefits were reduced when additional labor income was earned by the female head.

[10]Specifically, this "average" woman was assumed to be 24 years of age in 1976 and living

in a state that paid $308 in AFDC benefits in 1976. Furthermore, her 1968 family did not live in the South, and the female head of the 1968 family had 11 years of education.

[11]Although Levy's study appears to be the most thorough, it is important to note that two other studies of the intergenerational dynamics of welfare found no significant effects. Rein and Rainwater (1980) found that children of welfare families were no more likely to be receiving welfare income than children from lower-income families who had not received welfare. Not only did this relationship fail to show up among all split-off children, it also failed to emerge among the subgroup of split-off women with children. Using five years of data, Dickinson (1975) also found an insignificant effect of parental welfare receipt on children's welfare receipt. The approaches taken in these two studies differed from Levy's, making it difficult to reconcile the divergent findings.

[12]In some states, eligibility is extended to two-parent families when the father is unemployed.

[13]Elaborate experiments have been set up to examine work and family composition effects of an income maintenance program that extends potential benefits to all two-parent families. While those experiments do have a control group living within the present welfare system, for obvious ethical reasons they do not include a control group that is ineligible for any type of program.

[14]See Coe (1981) for a review of these studies.

[15]This statement is not strictly true, since it presumes that the absence of welfare payments would not have caused family members to draw more income from other sources. Evidence from other studies has shown that hours worked, and hence labor income, is affected by the receipt of welfare income—substantially for married women, moderately for women who head their own households, and very little for men.

[16]The estimate of one-year poverty (7.1 percent) in 1978 differs from the 6.8 percent estimate in Table 3.3 for reasons similar to those cited in footnote 15 of Chapter 2: a five-year look at the population must include those individuals who were alive for those five years, while a ten-year look must include the individuals living during that longer period. Children under the age of six in 1978 were a part of the five-year sample but not of the first five years of the ten-year period. Thus, the 7.1 percent estimate includes them, while the 6.8 percent estimate does not.

[17]These "prewelfare" poor are the same as those listed in Table 2.3 in Chapter 2.

[18]Although large numbers of the elderly poor are not entirely cut off from welfare programs many do not receive welfare benefits on a continuous basis. Rates of welfare receipt for persistently poor elderly were 91.3 percent and 63.9 percent, respectively, for at least one year and five years or more of welfare receipt. These rates are lower than the ones listed in Table 3.5 for the entire population.

[19]Many of the points raised in this section parallel ideas developed by Lane (1981) in his thoughtful discussion of the policy implications of Panel Study findings on welfare use patterns.

4

Dynamics of Work Hours, Unemployment, and Earnings

Labor income is the major ingredient in the economic status of most families and changes in family income most often reflect changes in labor income. Labor income is the product of two components: hours worked and hourly wage rates. We shall treat these two components separately in this chapter, beginning with an examination of the reported work hours of the adult men and women in the Panel Study, and then looking at patterns of earnings.

Many men reported working more than the standard "full-time" 40-hour week and, more important, very few of those surveyed worked a fairly constant number of hours from one year to the next. Work hours of women fluctuated a great deal from year to year, as these women moved into and out of the labor force or between part-time and full-time jobs. Surprisingly, however, the work hours of prime-age male workers fluctuated even more than those of women, owing primarily to variations in overtime, second jobs, or short periods of unemployment, rather than to disability or long-term unemployment. These fluctuations, coupled with the fact that the hourly earnings of men are both higher and more unstable than those of women, make the labor market earnings of men a considerably more volatile component of family income than the earnings of women.

Although many changes in work hours are voluntary, those due to unemployment usually are not.[1] When we look at the distribution and

95

consequences of unemployment among prime-age male household heads we find that roughly 10 percent report some unemployment in a given year, while nearly 40 percent were unemployed at least once in the decade between 1967 and 1976. On the average, unemployment compensation made up for about 25 percent of the earnings lost because of unemployment. Although occasional unemployment was quite widespread, chronic unemployment was not. Five percent of these household heads accounted for nearly half of the ten-year total unemployment. The chronically jobless were typically blue-collar workers with less than a high school education. Surprisingly, blacks were not overrepresented in the group of long-term unemployed.

The single most important—and most complex—labor market concept is the hourly wage rate. The second half of this chapter reviews some of the most prominent theories of wage rate determination and uses them to interpret patterns of wage level and change found among individuals in the Panel Study sample. The multiyear look at earnings afforded by the Panel Study is used in several ways. First, we averaged earnings over a period of ten years and examined the relationship between them and a set of characteristics of individual workers and their jobs. Educational attainment was found to be the most powerful determinant of earnings level—even after the effects of cognitive ability, motivation, and family background are taken into account. None of these measures was nearly as powerful as education in accounting for earnings differences among white men. Types of jobs were also important in determining workers' earnings, but a look at changes in earnings and the movement of workers in and out of different kinds of jobs suggests that they rarely become trapped in undesirable positions. There was little systematic relationship between substantial fluctuation of earnings from one year to the next and the type of job the worker held.

Patterns of Work Hours, 1969–1978

In the conventional view of work patterns, men are believed to work fairly stable 40-hour weeks, occasionally augmented by overtime and second jobs or decreased by unemployment. Women, on the other hand, are believed to show a more varied pattern, with some not working at all at a given time and with those who are employed often working considerably less than full time. But when we examine the actual work patterns of Panel Study individuals over the ten-year period between 1969 and 1978, we find that this picture, particularly for men, is not accurate.

Our analysis is based on the reported work hours of men and women living in their own households who were between the ages of 25 and 50 in the first of the ten years (1969).[2] These are the so-called "prime-age" workers—old enough to have been out of school for several years and to be living in their own households but not old enough by the end of the period to have reached the conventional early retirement age of 62 years.

Average Work Hours

Taking the ten-year period as a whole, the average work year for white men was considerably above the full-time 2,000 hour mark, as shown in the first column of Table 4.1.[3] Virtually none of these men had average work years so short that they could be regarded as completely out of the labor force throughout the entire period. Nearly half had average work years that were considerably more than full time (at least 2,250 hours).

Evidently second jobs and overtime work are quite prevalent. The Panel Study data do not distinguish between regular work hours and overtime hours, but they do show that more than half of the white men reported working at a second job at least once in the decade. Despite their generally heavy work years, more than half of the men reported at least once that they would have liked to have worked more.

Average annual work hours of black men were somewhat lower than those of white men—by about the equivalent of three 40-hour weeks. Black men were as likely as whites to have second jobs, but considerably more likely to report working fewer hours than they would have wished.

Patterns of work hours for women conform more closely to conventional wisdom. The average work year of both white and black women was less than 1,000 hours. This average includes women who were out of the labor force altogether, as well as those with full-time jobs. In a single year (1978 in this case), about two-fifths of all of the women in each racial group worked fewer than 250 hours, but not all of them were persistently employed for so few hours; only about one-fifth worked fewer than 250 hours in every one of the ten years. (These figures do not appear in Table 4.1.) So, while Census Bureau figures show that the overall fraction of women engaging in market work has edged upward in recent years, the number of women moving into and out of the labor force each year is quite large.[4] In contrast to men, very few women averaged more than 2,250 hours during the entire ten-year period, although roughly one-sixth of them worked that much in at least one of the ten years.

Table 4.1

AVERAGE ANNUAL WORK HOURS, 1969 TO 1978, FOR HOUSEHOLD HEADS AND WIVES AGE 25–50 IN 1969[a]

	Ten-Year Annual Average Work Hours	Percentage with 10-Year Average Annual Work Hours:				Percentage with 1 or More Years in which Work Hours Were:	
		Less than 250	Between 250 and 1750	Between 1750 and 2250	More than 2250	Less than 250	More than 2250
White men	2228 hours	1%	11%	43%	45%	10%	80%
Black men	2097	1	16	49	34	13	73
White women	854	33	48	17	2	72	17
Black women	931	29	55	14	2	68	17
All	1476 hours	18%	32%	29%	21%	44%	46%

[a]*Note:* The definition of "Household Heads and Wives" includes the unmarried women and the married or unmarried men who headed households, as well as the wives of men who headed households.
Table reads: "White men during the 1969–78 period averaged a 2228-hour work year. Only 1% of those white men averaged less than 250 hours."

Patterns of Changes in Work Hours

Because the labor income of household heads is usually the dominant source of family income, it is not surprising that changes in labor income were found to be the dominant component of change in total family income among families not undergoing major changes in composition (Duncan and Morgan, 1977). What is surprising, however, is that these changes in labor income were due almost as much to large changes in work hours as to changes in hourly wages.

Work hours were reported in each of the ten years, enabling us to calculate the amount of change between each two consecutive years and to average the total over the nine pairs of years.[5] This calculation is the average of the absolute value of change from one year to the next—e.g., both a decrease of 100 and an increase of 100 hours would count as 100. When this calculation was performed using the same group of prime-age men and women examined earlier, an astonishing amount of change was found—much more than can be attributed to reporting errors. Furthermore, changes in work hours of men actually exceed those of women.

Table 4.2 details these findings and shows that the average year-to-year change in work hours of men was more than 350 hours—about two months, in 40-hour weeks. Average change for women was not much less—280 hours for white women and about 320 hours for black women. No doubt some of this change is the artificial result of reporting errors, but these numbers are much too large to be attributed exclusively or even primarily to this factor. Nor can the comparatively larger changes for men be explained by reporting error; if anything, we would expect larger errors in the reports of the womens' work hours, since the work hours of married women were reported by their husbands.

A closer look at the distribution of change in work hours shows that large changes in hours (more than 500) were only slightly more frequent among men than women. A little over 20 percent of the white men reported work hours that changed by an average of more than 500 hours per year over the ten-year period, and nearly 75 percent experienced at least one year in which their work hours changed by at least that amount. For white and black women, the comparable percentages were only slightly lower. Women were much more likely than men to experience small changes (fewer than 100 hours).

The finding that yearly changes in work hours were usually larger for men than for women has important implications in assessing the causes of change in the economic status of families. It has long been known that

Table 4.2

YEAR-TO-YEAR CHANGES IN WORK HOURS, 1969 TO 1978, FOR HOUSEHOLD HEADS AND WIVES, AGE 25–50 IN 1969[a]

	Average Yearly Absolute Change in Work Hours	Percentage with Average Yearly Absolute Change in Work Hours:				Percentage for Whom Work Hours Changed by 500 Hours or More:	
		Less than 100	Between 100 and 250	Between 250 and 500	More than 500	At Least One Year	More than Half the Time
White men	358 hours	9%	31%	38%	22%	71%	14%
Black men	377	10	21	40	29	79	14
White women	280	28	24	31	17	65	9
Black women	318	26	18	33	23	68	10
All	319 hours	19%	27%	34%	20%	68%	11%

Note: The definition of "Household Heads and Wives" includes the unmarried women and the married or unmarried men who headed households, as well as the wives of men who headed households.

Table reads: "The average absolute value of the nine yearly changes in work hours between 1969 and 1978 was 358 hours for white men. Nine percent of the white men had average yearly changes amounting to less than 100 hours."

the labor income of the household head (defined as the husband in husband–wife families) is the principal component of the income of most families. It is commonly believed that this component is fairly stable and that changes in family income result more from fluctuations in other income sources, such as when a wife moves into and out of the labor force or from part-time to full-time work. Instead, the Panel Study data show large fluctuations in the work hours of prime age men. These fluctuations, coupled with the higher wage rates received by these men, result in very large year-to-year changes in labor income, changes that for most families are clearly larger than changes in other sources of income.

Explaining the Patterns

To what extent can we explain these dramatic fluctuations in work hours? Established economic theory presumes that each worker adjusts work hours and leisure to achieve the greatest possible total utility by trading the utility of the income earned from an additional hour of work against the utility lost by giving up leisure time in order to work that extra hour. Changes in work hours can be brought about by changes in wage rates and other sources of income, but two offsetting forces may be at work. The first, an income effect, predicts that any change that augments a worker's income (e.g., from winning a lottery, a decrease in taxes, or an increase in the wage rate) is likely induce that worker to work less and enjoy more leisure. The second, a substitution effect, predicts that increases in the amount earned per hour (e.g., from a decrease in tax rates or an increase in the wage rate) will make work hours more valuable and leisure more expensive, encouraging *more* work. But since these two effects—income and substitution—would offset one another, their net effect on work hours is ambiguous. Indeed, much of the debate about so-called "supply-side economics" centers on the likely response of workers to falling tax rates. Will workers respond to increased hourly take-home pay by working more hours, or will they use some of their added income to "buy" more leisure and thus work less? Economic theory cannot give a clear-cut answer to this question.

Can we find an answer by interpreting the pattern of changes in work hours exhibited by Panel Study household heads in light of these theoretical considerations?[6] One fact quickly emerges: There are pervasive constraints limiting most workers' ability to make the kinds of adjustments presumed by the theory. Dickinson (1974) found that only about one-eighth of employed male household heads in 1971 held jobs in which they were free to vary their work hours at well-defined rates of pay.[7] Some of the remaining seven-eighths reported being unable to work as much or as little as they would have liked, while others held salaried jobs where the pay rates for additional hours of work were unclear.[8]

The importance of these constraints in explaining changes in work hours was demonstrated by Morgan (1979). For household heads who reported working less than they would have liked in the first year but who were unconstrained in the second year, he found increases of about 40 hours in annual work hours from the first year to the second; and for household heads who reported working more than they would have liked in the first year and who were unconstrained in the second, he found decreases of about the same size.[9] Constraints resulting from unemployment or illness were even more important in explaining changes in work hours. Hours not worked because of unemployment or illness reduced annual work hours on an almost one-to-one basis. In other words, workers appeared unable (or unwilling) to compensate for these work-hour losses by taking on overtime work or second jobs during other times of the year.

What about the effect of changes in rates of pay on work hours? Here the evidence was quite clear: increases in rates of pay caused the number of work hours to decline substantially, suggesting that the income effect is considerably more important than the substitution effect.[10]

In addition to pervasive constraints on work hours, Morgan found that changes in work hours may well be influenced by income goals families set for themselves in response to changes in the rate of inflation and in their general standard of living. The combined work hours of the household heads and their wives increased significantly in years when inflation was high or when there was higher than average growth in the nation's real consumption. No well-developed theory incorporating constraints and income goals yet exists; such a theory might provide an important part of a complete understanding of the patterns of changing work hours.

The Incidence and Cost of Unemployment

The most familiar indicator of joblessness is the monthly unemployment rate. Gathered from a cross-sectional survey of the population each month, the unemployment rate shows what fraction of the labor force had unsuccessfully sought work in the previous four weeks.[11] Month-to-month changes in the unemployment rate are used as indicators of the economic health of the nation. But, as with other cross-sectional measures, the unemployment rate is woefully inadequate as an indicator of the underlying dynamics of unemployment or of the distribution of hardship caused by the economy's inability to generate enough jobs. An unchanging unemployment rate could, for example, result if a large proportion of workers spend some time unemployed each month but individually experience only relatively small decreases in their total work time and income. Or, conversely, an unchanging rate might result if a small proportion of workers experience persistent or recurrent unemployment and major decreases in income. These two scenarios are very different in terms of the distribution and severity of the unemployment burden, and the policies appropriate to each would also differ dramatically.

In this section, Panel Study data on the 10-year unemployment experiences of prime-age men are used to describe the incidence and economic costs of unemployment. Specifically, the information comes from male household heads who were age 26–55 in 1967 and is based on the analysis presented in Corcoran and Hill (1979) and in Hill and Corcoran (1979). Although these prime-age men have substantially lower unemployment rates than other subgroups—in particular, women and younger workers—they do constitute a large segment of the total, and many are the sole wage earners in their families.

The pattern of annual unemployment for these men, shown by the dashed line in Figure 4.1, reflects changes in the economy's overall level of unemployment, rising substantially during the recessionary periods of 1970–71 and 1974–76.[12] The longer duration of unemployment spells during these periods increased the economic costs of unemployment as well. The solid line in Figure 4.1 shows the fraction of disposable income lost by those who had experienced at least some unemployment. "Lost disposable income" is defined as lost after-tax earnings less whatever unemployment compensation may have been received. Although it is possible to construct cases in which tax-free unemployment benefits can enable an unemployed worker to maintain nearly the same economic status as when he was working, Panel Study data for 1976 show that, on the average, unemployment compensation made up only about one-quarter of the lost after-tax earnings (Corcoran and Hill, 1979, p. 20). As a result, unemployed workers were left with 10 to 25 percent less disposable income than if they had not become unemployed.

A look at the ten-year unemployment experiences of these same workers shows a much greater incidence but somewhat less financial loss. Nearly 40 percent of these prime-age men were unemployed at

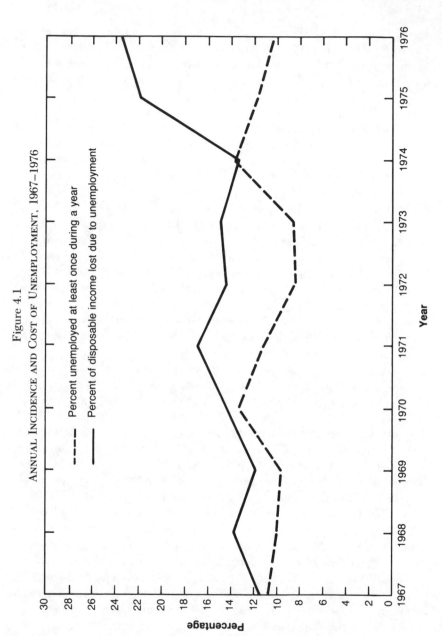

Figure 4.1
ANNUAL INCIDENCE AND COST OF UNEMPLOYMENT, 1967–1976

Table 4.3

CHARACTERISTICS OF CHRONICALLY UNEMPLOYED MALE HOUSEHOLD HEADS,
1967–1976

Characteristics in 1976	Workers with 64 or More Weeks of Unemployment in the 1967–76 Period	All Male Household Heads
Education:		
Less than high school	59%	31%
High school	31	33
At least some college	10	36
Type of Job:		
Blue-collar occupation	80	46
Construction industry	43	10
Black	6	7
Age:		
Under age 45	39	36
Age 45–54	40	43
Age 55–64	21	21
Union member	42	31
Total	5.1%	100%

Table reads: "Almost three-fifths (59%) of the long-term unemployed male household heads had less than a high school education; 31% of all male household heads had less than a high school education."

least once during the ten years, and the average amount of disposable income lost by the unemployed was more than $5,000. Expressed as a percentage of total disposable income, however, this loss amounted to only about 4 percent.

Despite the widespread incidence of unemployment over the ten-year period, the burden of unemployment during those years was quite unevenly distributed. About 5 percent of those men who were unemployed at some time accounted for nearly half of the work lost by the entire group, averaging 96 weeks of unemployment and $19,114 in lost disposable income over the ten years—or about 15 percent of their expected ten-year earnings.

Who were such men who experienced these large losses of work and money as a result of unemployment? Table 4.3 suggests that long-run unemployment was concentrated disproportionately among high school dropouts, among workers in blue-collar occupations, and among workers in the construction industry. While only 31 percent of all male household heads had less than a high school education, nearly 60 percent of the long-term unemployed had not completed high school.[13] Eighty percent of the chronically unemployed were blue-collar workers and 43 percent of them had been working in some capacity in the construction industry. Surprisingly, blacks were not overrepresented among the long-term unemployed household heads.[14]

Patterns of Earnings, 1969–1978

Theories of Earnings

Many theories of earnings have been advanced, each emphasizing some aspect of the individual worker (e.g., skills, ability, motivation, social class) or of labor market structure (e.g., occupational hierarchy, discrimination). The explanation most widely accepted today among economists is the human capital theory, which focuses on the individual worker and the skills he or she brings to the labor market. Jobs themselves play a minor role in this theory; their main function is to provide workers with a way in which work skills can be given their proper economic reward. Although it may take time to find the best match between workers and jobs, the theory presumes jobs to be freely available to anyone possessing the qualifying skills. A contrasting view of the labor market is provided by a much less extensively and rigorously developed collection of explanations called "segmented" or "dual/internal" labor market theories. They focus on the demand, or employer side of the labor market and are predicated on the existence of institutional constraints and other impediments to a freely competitive labor market. Since much of the analysis presented here and in Chapters 5 and 6 is based on these theories, in particular the human capital theory, it is worth reviewing some of their more salient features.

Human capital theory. Put forth in its current form by Schultz (1961) and Becker (1975), the human capital model views earnings as a monetary return on the bundle of skills (human capital) that each worker brings to the labor market. The key assumptions are that the process of acquiring skills is under the control of the individual worker and that it is a costly process. Although many kinds of activities can increase a worker's productivity, proponents of the human capital model have held that the primary determinants of an individual's rate of pay are investments in schooling and on-the-job training. On-the-job training is based on the recognition that learning does not cease with the completion of formal schooling. In fact, it is usually asserted that many, if not most, important job skills are learned primarily on the job, so at some point it simply becomes more efficient to transfer the site of learning to the labor market. Such learning in conjunction with work is what the human capital model calls investment in on-the-job training.

The costs of investing in post-secondary formal education are the most obvious: In addition to explicit costs in the form of tuition payments, students incur the implicit costs of foregoing income they might have earned had they been working rather than in school. But learning on the job, according to the human capital model, also exacts a price in that workers receive lower wages during the period when training is demanding time and perhaps other resources that might otherwise be devoted to production. That is, since workers who are being trained on the job produce less than workers who are not, a competitive labor market would pay job trainees less than they would earn if, instead, they took similar jobs that did not provide additional training.[15] An individual may choose the lower-paying job as an investment in on-the-job training promising higher overall future earnings than could be expected from an initially better-paying job that provides no additional training.

If individuals are free to determine the volume and timing of their self-investment in human capital in order to maximize their lifetime earnings, then most will find it advantageous to make the investment early, in order to earn more over the greatest number of years. As a result, individuals' investment costs will be relatively high during their first few working years; their early labor earnings will be depressed. Their subsequent labor earnings will rise sharply at first and then more gradually, as the optimal rate of investment declines and the returns on previous investments are received.

Institutional theories. A collection of alternative explanations of earnings determination have been proposed, many of them stressing the characteristics of jobs and job markets, rather than of individuals holding those jobs. Prominent among these theories is the notion of a "dual" labor market, split into a primary sector and a secondary sector, with little worker mobility between the two sections (Doeringer and Piore, 1971). Jobs in the primary sector are desirable in that they offer steady employment, higher wages, and better promotion opportunities. They have developed in stable, high-wage industries through a process in which customary work rules and practices, frequently formalized by collective bargaining agreements, have established a separate market for those already hired (Kerr, 1954). Only workers who have gained access to these jobs via a limited number of "ports of entry" at the lower steps of promotion ladders are considered for the higher rungs.

Proponents of a dual labor market theory believe that only certain jobs can be characterized in this way. Jobs not part of the primary sector "tend to have low wages and fringe benefits, poor working conditions, higher turnover, little chance of advancement, and often arbitrary and capricious supervision" (Doeringer and Piore, 1971, pp. 165–66).

The dual labor market theorists do acknowledge the importance of on-the-job training, but they interpret it differently than do the proponents of the human capital theory. In the dual labor market view, training is largely a matter of technological determinism which influences the design of all jobs so that any given job will involve some specified amount and period of training. Thus the training that individuals may acquire on the job will be determined by the jobs to which they gain access. This technological determinism differs from the human capital view in assuming that individuals cannot choose freely among jobs because of the presumed restrictions on mobility (particularly between the primary and secondary sectors) that are central to the dual labor market model.

In practice, analysis along these lines has tended to focus on the labor market problems of low-wage urban workers, especially blacks. It is usually argued that labor market discrimination tends to confine disproportionate numbers of blacks to secondary-sector jobs from which it is difficult to escape to the better jobs in the primary sector.

Although the human capital and institutional theories differ dramatically in their assumptions about the nature of the labor market, it has proved quite difficult to formulate sharp empirical tests of either, especially with data on a cross section of workers at a single point in time. Measures of one of the key variables in human capital theory—on-the-job training—are seldom available. Much of the empirical work on the relationship between training and earnings has taken the indirect and potentially circular route of inferring patterns of training from information on earnings. Tests of the institutional theories have been hampered by a lack of consensus on a classification of jobs by sector. Both theories have generally been tested using cross-sectional data, even though both make many predictions about the temporal patterns of earnings and jobs.

Information from longitudinal surveys in general and the Panel Study in particular are well suited for analyzing earnings in light of these theories. Panel Study information comes from a recent, representative national sample of individuals, and it provides rich detail on the background, attitudes, skills, and job characteristics of the respondents. The longitudinal design of the study provides a view of the average level of earnings as well as information on changes in earnings over time.

Determinants of Ten-Year Average Earnings

There have been many attempts to understand the ways in which background, attitudes, and schooling affect occupation and earnings. Although some of them use data that are in some respects better suited to the task than ours, the relative strengths of the Panel Study data lie in providing a better picture of the permanent economic status individuals have attained and in containing a set of personality measures rarely found in a single national cross-sectional study. These features can be used to describe results that are consistent with most of the more sophisticated work on models of earnings determination.[16]

This section focuses on the ability of skills, attitudes, and job characteristics to explain the differences in ten-year average earnings observed for a representative sample of white men. Specifically, the analysis is performed on a group of white male household heads between the ages of 25 and 50 in 1969 who worked at least 500 hours in each of the years between 1969 and 1978.[17] The structure of earnings differences between white and black men is detailed in Chapter 5, while Chapter 6 examines differences in earnings between men and women.

Although a factor such as education or motivation may prove to be related to earnings, that relationship in itself does not explain *how* such a factor operates to influence earnings. For example, using Panel Study data, we find that differences in the level of education can account for a substantial share of the long-run earnings differences between individual workers. But is it because education provides valued skills? Or is it because the level of education itself is determined by such other causal factors as an individual's motivation, capabilities, or family background? To help determine the precise role education plays, it would be necessary to assess the explanatory power of different levels of education of individuals who are otherwise similar in ability, motivation, and family backgrounds. Further, even if such an assessment established that those with more education earn more because they have acquired more job-related skills, it does not automatically follow that an investment in education is profitable. The potential profit depends on whether such benefits as increased earnings are greater than the costs of acquiring further education. Thus, in simply establishing the explanatory power of a measure such as education in determining earnings, we have addressed only one of the many important issues surrounding wage determination.

The process by which earnings are ultimately determined may be considered part of an overall sequence of life events. In this sequence, each individual is born with a specific genetic endowment and spends childhood in home environments over which he or she has little control. These homes differ widely in the advantages they offer. Such factors as the amount of time and money parents bestow on their children, as well as differences in the environment outside the home, can lead to substantial differences in the attitudes and cognitive skills acquired by children as well as in the amounts and types of formal skills, principally schooling, that they will ultimately bring to the labor market. All of these variables, operating through their effects on choices of occupation and location, affect earnings.

As a first step in our analysis, we relate the ten-year average hourly earnings of these men to the set of personal characteristics shown in Table 4.4. Job variables have not been included at this stage. The columns of numbers show the fraction of the variation of earnings that can be accounted for before ("unadjusted") and after ("adjusted") the effects of the other measures have been taken into account statistically. Several important facts emerge from this analysis—facts that are consistent with findings of more detailed studies.

First and foremost is the impressive ability of education to explain permanent earnings differences between individuals. About one-fifth of the variation in hourly earnings is explained by schooling level, an

Table 4.4

FRACTION OF VARIANCE
IN TEN-YEAR AVERAGE HOURLY EARNINGS OF WHITE MEN
ACCOUNTED FOR BY SCHOOLING, ATTITUDES, AND BACKGROUND

Measure	Unadjusted Fraction of Variance Explained	Adjusted[a] Fraction of Variance Explained
Years of education	20%	15%
Years of work experience	3	3
Test score	10	2
Achievement motivation	4	1
Father's education	4	1
Efficacy	3	1

[a]*Note:* Adjusted fractions of variance explained are obtained from a multiple regression that includes all other listed variables plus region and city size.
Table reads: "Taken by themselves, differences in years of education account for 20% of the variation in average hourly earnings. Among individuals with similar amounts of work experience, test scores, attitudes, etc., differences in years of education account for 15% of that variation."

amount twice as large as any of the other characteristics on the list.[18] The more-educated individuals have usually acquired more valuable job skills in school, but they differ from the less-educated in other important ways as well. If the effect of education on earnings is really merely a reflection of the fact that the more-educated are more capable (test score), or more motivated (achievement motivation), or have a greater sense of the effectiveness of their own actions (efficacy), or come from more advantaged backgrounds (father's education), then the ability of education to explain earnings differences between individuals with similar capabilities, motivation, efficacy, and background ought to be very low. But when differences in these other traits are taken into account statistically, education retains much of its explanatory power. The "adjusted" fraction of the variation in earnings explained by differences in schooling levels is still an impressive 15 percent. The unadjusted and adjusted pattern of education effects, shown in Figure 4.2, indicates a fairly steady rise in hourly earnings over the entire education range.

Of course, we cannot rule out the possibility that *unmeasured* factors may account for the education effects or the possibility that the personality and background measures included here are measured too imprecisely to adjust adequately for their effects. However, on the basis of the adjustments that can be made, educational attainment is clearly the most powerful characteristic in distinguishing white men with high from those with low long-run average earnings. The fact that the explanatory power of education persists even when differences in attitudes, cognitive ability, and background are taken into account provides strong support for the human capital theory which gives such a central role to education.[19]

A second noteworthy result that emerges here, as well as in more sophisticated studies of earnings based on Panel Study data, is the modest effect of the measures of cognitive ability and personality traits. Taken by itself, the score on a thirteen-question test of cognitive ability accounted for about 10 percent of the variation in average hourly earnings. After adjusting for the effects of the other measures, most notably education, the explanatory power of the test score measure falls to 2 percent—much less than that found for education, although still a highly significant result in a statistical sense. Thus, the conventional wisdom that links cognitive ability and success (e.g., "if you're so smart, why aren't you rich?") appears misguided. A more important implication of the weak link between intelligence and economic success, developed at some length by Bowles and Gintis (1972-73), is the irrelevance of much

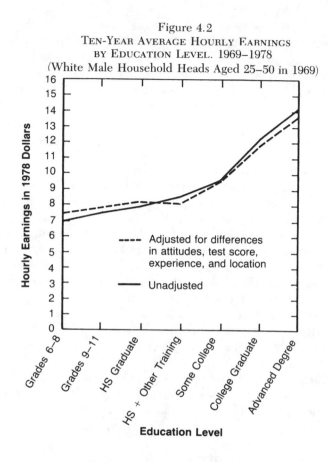

Figure 4.2
TEN-YEAR AVERAGE HOURLY EARNINGS
BY EDUCATION LEVEL. 1969–1978
(White Male Household Heads Aged 25–50 in 1969)

of the recent debate regarding the heritability of intelligence. The unstated assumption in much of that debate is that one's intelligence is the principal determinant of economic success. This simply does not appear to be the case.[20]

As with cognitive ability, the measures of achievement motivation and efficacy failed to account for much of the permanent earnings difference between individuals. Bearing in mind that these measures, too, may be only distantly related to the actual existence and nature of these personality traits in the respondents, there nevertheless seems to be little evidence that personality differences can account for many of the observed earnings differences.

A third result of interest is the pattern of average earnings for workers

Figure 4.3
TEN-YEAR AVERAGE HOURLY EARNINGS
BY YEARS OF LABOR FORCE EXPERIENCE, 1969–1978
(White Male Household Heads Aged 25–50 in 1969)

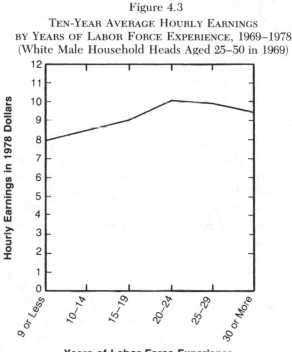

Years of Labor Force Experience

with different amounts of labor force experience. Figure 4.3 shows the pattern of rising earnings for white workers over much of the life cycle.[21] This pattern can be interpreted in several ways. Proponents of the human capital theory attribute rising earnings to individual investments in on-the-job training; in that view, workers forego earnings when they are just starting out in order to acquire valuable job skills. Since their payoff period for these investments is longest, the youngest workers are apt to make the heaviest investments (take the lowest wages) and will thus exhibit more rapid subsequent increases in earnings.[22] Alternative explanations give much more weight to institutional factors such as seniority or to informational problems in the market that make it a time-consuming process to sort workers into jobs for which they are best-suited.[23]

The final measure in Table 4.4, the amount of schooling of the individual's father, is often used as an imprecise measure of family background. By itself, the level of father's education accounts for about 4 percent of the variation in earnings. Much of this power is dissipated when adjustments are made for the effects of the other variables, again most notably the individual's own level of education. Thus, parental status operates to affect children's status primarily by determining the level of education of the child.

Corcoran and Datcher (1981) performed a much more elaborate investigation of the importance of background factors on individual earnings. They found that an extensive list of socioeconomic background variables explained about 14 percent of the variance in hourly earnings for a group of young male household heads. Religion and the income level of the parental family (rather than their education or occupational attainment) were the two most important predictors in the group of background variables. Jews had higher hourly earnings than Catholics, and Protestants had lower hourly earnings than either of the other two groups, even after differences in educational attainment and other family background factors had been taken into account.

An alternative strategy for estimating the effect of family background is to compare siblings. The earnings of brothers may be more similar than the earnings of individuals chosen randomly from the population as a whole because of their shared heredity, shared family background, shared experiences of being raised in the same community and sent to the same school, and for other reasons as well. Using this method, Corcoran and Datcher (1981) found that shared family background accounted for nearly one-third of the variation in hourly earnings—an amount that changed little when adjustments were made for differences in educational attainment. The discrepancy between the explanatory power of the direct measures of background and the indirect method using similarities between brothers has not yet been resolved satisfactorily, but it does suggest that family background may be considerably more powerful in determining economic success than past studies using direct background measures have indicated.

The bundle of attitudes, skills, and experience workers bring to the labor market are translated into earnings through jobs. Knowledge of an individual's occupation and industry sector adds substantially to one's ability to explain his or her earnings—even when the effects of personal characteristics have been taken into account. Before adjusting for the effects of other factors, simple ten-category classifications of occupation and industry account for 20 percent and 7 percent, respectively, of the variation in ten-year average hourly earnings of white men. When these two variables plus an indicator of union status are added to the set of predictors shown in Table 4.4, the fraction of variation in earnings explained by the complete set of variables increases from 36 percent to 43 percent. Workers in the highest-status white-collar occupations—professionals and managers—generally earn more than the average for individuals with similar measured characteristics, while workers in the lowest status occupations—laborers, for example—earn considerably less. Not surprisingly, unionized workers earn more than their nonunion counterparts working in similar jobs, and jobs in certain industries, in particular manufacturing, pay more than average as well. These patterns suggest that jobs themselves affect earnings independent of the personal characteristics of workers, giving some support to an institutional view. This is examined in more detail in the following section.

Life-Cycle Changes in Earnings

Since for many years social scientists have had to rely on data from cross-sectional studies, there is considerably more research evidence to explain the differences in earnings among a group of individuals observed at a single point in time than to explain changes in the earnings of a single individual over a period of time. Despite the limited evidence available, both the human capital and the segmented labor market theories have been formulated as models describing the path of individual workers' earnings over time. Even the most basic information about the kind of individual, year-to-year changes that actually occurred for a representative sample of workers was generally unavailable until the Panel and National Longitudinal Studies were well underway. Do an individual's earnings tend to be stable over time? Do better-educated workers tend to receive regular increases in earnings? Is there an identifiable group of workers whose employment and earnings fluctuate erratically? Do life-cycle earnings patterns appear to be the result of investments in training?

Economists have answered these questions only indirectly, through analyses of cross-sectional data on earnings differences observed at a given time for a sample of workers of different ages or work experience. These patterns are depicted in Figure 4.3. By contrast, Panel Study data provide longitudinal information on earnings of individuals over time, allowing us to address the above questions directly.

In the following, Panel Study data are used to describe the typical earnings changes that an individual experiences throughout his working life, and these changes are examined in light of the various theories of earnings determination. As in the previous section, the focus here is on the hourly wage rates of white male household heads (age 25 to 50 in 1969) over the ten-year period from 1969 to 1978.

Patterns of Ten-Year Changes in Earnings

The first and most basic question concerning the course of individual earnings is whether they are relatively stable over time. Do high-wage earners remain high-wage earners? Are low-wage earners locked into their situation? If "good jobs" and "bad jobs" represent two distinctly separate labor market sectors (the institutional theory), one's current earnings should be a good predictor of one's future position. If, however, low earnings reflect the temporary status of, for example, a person acquiring on-the-job training, then an individual's earnings position might change substantially from low to high over a period of years (the human capital theory). As was done for family income in Chapter 1, we can examine changes in relative earnings position with a transition table, ranking the population of white working adult men in 1969 according to their 1969 wage rates, and dividing them into five equal groups (quintiles). Following a similar procedure with data taken ten years later in 1978, a transition table is constructed to show what fractions of those surveyed experienced various changes in quintile position between 1969 and 1978. This is shown in Table 4.5. The underlined numbers are the proportion of those who did not change their relative earnings position; "rags to riches" changes appear in the upper right portion of the table, and "riches to rags" changes are shown in the bottom left corner.[24]

Table 4.5 shows that the relative earnings positions of white men are subject to a great deal of change. Less than half (44 percent—the sum of the underlined numbers on the table) of all of these men were in the same wage quintile in 1978 that they had occupied in 1969, and one person in five changed position by two quintiles or more. Consider, for example, individuals who were in the middle (third quintile) of the wage distribution in 1969; ten years later, only about 30 percent (6.7/21.6) were still in that same quintile. Another 30 percent of them had improved their position and, indeed, about 8 percent of the original middle-quintile wage earners had moved all the way to the top fifth of the wage distribution. Finally, 40 percent of these individuals slipped to a lower earnings position, and one in seven (3.1/21.6) fell all the way to the bottom quintile.

These changes in position are slightly more common for the three middle quintiles, but there is a substantial amount of relative improvement and decline even at the top and bottom. Of the lowest-wage workers in 1969, just over 50 percent were still in the bottom quintile, while almost 25 percent had moved up to at least the third quintile.

Table 4.5

ESTIMATED FRACTIONS OF WHITE MEN IN VARIOUS COMBINATIONS OF
1969 AND 1978 HOURLY EARNINGS QUINTILES
(All White Male Household Heads, Age 25–50 in 1969)

Hourly Earnings Quintile in 1969	Hourly Earnings Quintile in 1978					All
	Lowest	Fourth	Third	Second	Highest	
Lowest	9.5%	4.0%	2.7%	0.9%	0.7%	17.8%
Fourth	4.6	7.3	3.9	3.2	1.0	19.9%
Third	3.1	5.2	6.7	4.8	1.8	21.6%
Second	1.0	2.0	3.7	8.2	5.1	20.0%
Highest	0.8	1.0	2.2	3.9	12.5	20.5%
All	19.0%	19.5%	19.3%	21.0%	21.1%	100.0%

Table reads: "Just 9.5% of working white men earned so little in both 1969 and 1978 that they placed in the lowest hourly income quintile for both those years."

Stability of position was greatest for the top quintile, but even here, only about 60 percent were still in their original position, and about 20 percent of this group fell into the bottom three quintiles in 1978.

Similar results emerge when changes in quintile position are studied for annual earnings rather than hourly wage rates. About 45 percent of these white men maintained the same income quintile position in 1969 and 1978 and just under 20 percent moved at least two quintiles.

It is quite probable that some of the observed earnings mobility of individuals over time is actually due to errors in either reporting or coding, since there are acknowledged problems of obtaining accurate information on income and no study can completely eliminate these errors. Measurement error is particularly important in analyzing change since almost any error will create the appearance of change. However, although it would certainly be a mistake to ignore completely the role of measurement error, there are reasons to believe that much of the mobility shown in Table 4.5 is genuine. First, the income information in the Panel Study is the result of a series of tested questions and comes from respondents who have repeatedly given us their cooperation. Second, a similar study using earnings information reported by employers to the Social Security Administration—and thus presumably less prone to errors—found similar changes in relative earnings.[25]

Black workers experienced relative earnings changes similar to those for whites even though they are more heavily represented in the lower earnings quintiles. In all, more than half of the black workers in this age range changed quintile position between 1969 and 1978. About one-third of them improved their relative position, and almost half of those who began in the lowest quintile ended up in higher quintiles.

The extent and pattern of earnings changes shown in Table 4.5, as well as similar changes found for black workers, do not support the institutional labor market model. After all, many of those in the lowest quintile in 1969 experienced a great deal of relative improvement; only about half of the workers of either race who were in the lowest quintile in 1978 had been in that position in 1969. These findings are somewhat more consistent with the human capital model, since it predicts that some individuals who are low earners in one year may have a much more favorable position later on if they invest heavily in on-the-job training. But, of course, since these simple transition tables don't tell us *why* some individuals did so much better and others much worse, this support for the human capital model is very indirect. What we do know is that the earnings position of an individual in any given year is not a very permanent one.

Along with earnings mobility, there also appears to be a corresponding amount of movement over time of workers among jobs and even different sectors of the economy. The Panel Study data do not support the contention of the dual labor market model that there is extremely low mobility out of secondary sector jobs. Although there is still no consensus about the classification of jobs in the primary and secondary sectors, we can gain a rough sense of intersector mobility if we assume that the secondary sector consists of all clerical and sales workers, unskilled laborers, and nonunion operatives who work in nondurable manufacturing (textiles, paper products, etc.). Using that classification scheme to identify secondary workers in 1971 and again in 1978, it was found that employment in the secondary sector was not a permanent condition. Of the white men who held secondary sector positions in 1971, only about half were still there after seven years. For black men, who are usually thought of as more apt to be employed in the secondary sector, there was only a little more permanence to secondary sector status. About 40 percent of the black males who were in secondary sector jobs in 1971 were no longer in that category by 1978. Although this analysis is imprecise and the classification scheme is debatable, the findings are supported by a detailed and thorough study by Andrisani (1976). In his analysis of the National Longitudinal Study data on job changes for young male workers he concludes that "there do not appear to be impenetrable boundaries separating two broadly defined market sectors" (Andrisani, 1976, p.18).

Patterns of Yearly Change

Year-to-year changes in earnings are as interesting to observe as longer-run changes in position. Are earnings changes generally small and gradual or large and erratic? Do they appear to be the result of investments in training, or a result of promotions through internal labor markets? Or are earnings heavily influenced by such factors as unemployment, illness, availability of overtime or a second job, or the general state of the economy, and therefore partly beyond a worker's control? Have workers been able to keep up with inflation? These questions are important not only for understanding the situations of workers and their families, but, once again, for evaluating the underlying economic theories of earnings determination.

The Panel Study information on the pattern of yearly changes in individual earnings (Hoffman, 1977b) is diverse and surprising. On the whole, earnings over a worker's career exhibit a general upward trend; this was true even in the chaotic, inflationary economic environment of the 1970s and undoubtedly has continued to characterize the early 1980s. But underlying that trend is a tremendous amount of year-to-year fluctuation in earnings, both upward and downward. No identifiable group—not the more educated, not union members, not even higher-income persons—seems to be immune from these changes in year-to-year income. There is no evidence that there are secure, protected niches in the economy. Once again, we find that variability rather than stability and regularity characterizes the working lives of most men.

One common notion is that wage increases for most workers in the 1970s failed to keep up with inflation. Falling standards of living are generally supposed to be the plight of many American households. According to surveys by the Department of Labor, the median earnings of wage and salary workers have fallen in the past decade. However, those survey results are potentially quite unrepresentative of what happens to a group of experienced workers over time,[26] and, in fact, results from the Panel study suggest that most workers experienced rising, not falling, real wages. After adjusting for the effects of inflation, we found that nearly two-thirds of these workers had higher wages in 1978 than they had ten years earlier. For 40 percent of all workers, real earnings rose by 25 percent or more. Some others did fare poorly—about 15 percent of all workers had real earnings in 1978 that were at least 25 percent lower than they had been in 1969. Older workers did somewhat worse than younger ones.

Although the trend for most workers is upward, the amount of year-to-year change in earnings for individuals is very large and quite irregular. Consider a typical worker whose real earnings increased by 20 to 30 percent from 1969 to 1978. This total change could have come from steady and regular increases each year of between 2 and 3 percent, or from much larger amounts of upward and downward change. A process of gradual change turns out to be exceedingly rare. For the white men in the sample, the absolute change in hourly wages from one year to the next averaged not 3 percent or even 10 percent, but 28 percent. Averages can, of course, be dominated by a few large changes, but in this case, large changes were widely distributed among individuals. Fewer than 1 percent of these workers had wages that were so stable from one year to the next that their average change in yearly earnings over the ten-year period amounted to 10 percent or less. And only about 30 percent had average yearly increases of 20 percent or less.

Of course, not all of these changes in earnings were increases, since nine years of increases in excess of 25 percent would make even a low-wage worker quite well off. In the more common pattern of earnings change, large increases are followed by partially offsetting declines, moderate enough to preserve the overall upward trend, but large enough to generate the enormous variability observed in earnings.

Table 4.6 provides some details on the actual pattern of earnings changes. It shows the distribution of white male household heads according to the number of years (out of nine years) in which hourly and annual earnings had increased from the previous year and the number of years in which the change in earnings (either upward or down) was 10 percent or more. In both cases, wage comparisons are made after allowing for the effects of inflation. The almost universal incidence of large wage changes and of occasional wage declines is clear from Table 4.6. Virtually all of these white men had at least one wage change greater than 10 percent and at least one year in which wages were the same or lower than in the previous year. Most people experienced much more change and many more declines than that. About half the sample had year-to-year wage changes in excess of 10 percent in at least six of the nine years, and more than half experienced a decline in their real wage in four or more years. Only a small fraction had steady, regular increases. About 14 percent had decreases in only two years or less. Only about half that number (7.6 percent) had two or fewer years in which their earnings changed by less than 10 percent from the preceding year.

The annual income for these individuals was slightly more stable, but

Table 4.6

DISTRIBUTION OF WORKING WHITE MEN ACCORDING TO NUMBER OF YEARS
WITH VARIOUS CHANGES IN EARNINGS (1969–1978)

Earnings Event	Number of Years with Changes					
	0	1–2	3–4	5–6	7–8	9
Real hourly earnings increased	0.0%	0.2%	23.0%	63.2%	13.7%	0.0%
Real hourly earnings rose or fell by more than 10%	0.0	7.6	24.2	34.7	28.1	5.3
Real annual earnings increased	0.0	1.1	23.9	60.3	14.6	0.0
Real annual income rose or fell by more than 10%	0.0	16.5	28.3	30.7	21.0	3.3

Table reads: "None (0.0%) of the working white men had no year-to-year increases in real hourly earnings during the 1969–1978 period."

only in comparison with their hourly wages. The average year-to-year change in annual income was slightly lower for their hourly wages—25 percent versus 28 percent—and the fraction with average changes of 20 percent or less was also lower. Large year-to-year changes in annual income were not quite so common. While half of all individuals saw their hourly earnings change at least six times by 10 percent or more, this was true of the annual income of about 40 percent of these men. But, as Table 4.6 shows, year-to-year increases in annual earnings followed almost the same pattern as did increases in hourly wages. No individual completely escaped a decline in earnings, and almost 60 percent had declines in at least four years.

These patterns of life-cycle changes in individual earnings do not support the dual labor market concepts of a protected primary sector and a rigid secondary sector. The human capital model, with its emphasis on investment in training, does predict the observed upward trend in individual earnings over time and can accommodate some of the changes in relative earnings position that were discussed above. But consistency with the basic model would seem to require much more regular and moderate earnings changes than the changes that actually occurred.[27]

It is possible that these theories might characterize some special subgroups of the population better than others. Perhaps there are some individuals who enjoy modest and regular real wage increases in most years, whose earnings profiles conform to patterns expected from investment in training or a job in the primary sector. There is no definitive way to examine this possibility, since the set of possible groups of individuals is endless. But a more detailed look at the Panel Study data (Hoffman, 1977b) found nothing even approaching regular increases in real wages or annual income for the more educated, for those in unions, or for those in the most skilled occupations. The only factor that was somewhat successful in distinguishing workers with more increases was age. Increases for younger workers were somewhat more frequent than those for older workers—a fact broadly consistent with the human capital theory's prediction that younger workers make larger and more frequent investments in on-the-job training, and inconsistent with the dual labor market's prediction that older, rather than younger, workers would tend to be found in the more secure primary sector jobs. But these age-related differences were not great—more than half of even the youngest workers experienced decreases in at least three of the nine years.[28]

Summary

A longitudinal look at the work hours and the earnings of prime-age workers reveals remarkable volatility in both. The average difference in hours worked from one year to the next amounted to more than six 40-hour weeks for women and, surprisingly, even more for men. Some of these year-to-year changes were produced by entry into the labor force or departure from it altogether (and undoubtedly some were the result of errors in the reporting and transcribing of the hours), but many changes, especially for men, resulted from changes in the length of the standard work week, in overtime hours and second jobs, and from short spells of unemployment. Hourly earnings also changed markedly from one year to the next, by an average of 25 percent for prime-age men. Fluctuating work hours and hourly earnings of family heads produced most of the instability in family income that was noted in Chapter 1 for families not undergoing fundamental changes in composition. The movement of married women into and out of the labor force or from part-time to full-time jobs had a lesser impact on family income, principally because their hourly earnings were so much lower than their husbands'.

Describing the fluctuations in work hours is much easier than explaining why they came about; decisions regarding work hours are made in an environment of institutional constraints. Many workers reported being unable to work as much as they would like. Work hours appeared to fall in response to increases in hourly earnings but to rise in response to both increases in consumption standards for the nation as a whole and to higher than average rates of inflation as workers set and adjust their income goals. However, the task of explaining the observed changes in light of economic (and perhaps psychological) theories has only just begun.

Similarly, tests of theories developed to explain why some workers earn so much more than others have only recently begun changing from cross-sectional data on different workers at a single point in time to panel information on the earnings of the same individuals over an extended period. Our look at the ten-year average earnings of a cross section of prime-aged men confirmed many of the findings from prior studies: educational attainment is relatively powerful in distinguishing individuals with different levels of earnings, while attitudes and a simple measure of cognitive ability are not. Furthermore, the power of education is diminished only slightly by taking into account the fact that the more highly educated also tend to have the most advantaged backgrounds. When one also considers the evidence presented in Chapter 1 that education confers an ability to escape many unfortunate life events, educational attainment emerges as the single most important determinant of economic status. Although several reasons might be offered to account for the impact of education, we tend to favor an explanation centered on the skills developed through education, rather than on educational credentials or on the attitudes or backgrounds of those who receive the most schooling.

Important as it is, however, educational attainment can account for only about one-sixth of the earnings differences among prime-age white men. Earnings also differ systematically, but to a smaller degree, among workers with various amounts of work experience and different backgrounds and attitudes. Better measurement of these factors might increase their explanatory power considerably. Work experience is an imperfect indicator of the human capital skills that workers acquire through on-the-job training. An extensive list of family background measures cannot account for a large share of the earnings differences observed among brothers with a common family background. Much work remains to be done to develop more refined measures of these underlying factors.

The knowledge that might be acquired through increasingly refined analyses of earnings observed for cross-sections of workers could well be dwarfed by the knowledge gained from an examination of the year-to-year changes in the earnings of the same workers. Although longitudinal analysis is still in its infancy, even its most basic descriptive findings are revealing. The fact that very few male workers appear to be locked into a given economic position, coupled with the movement found from "bad" jobs to "good" ones, contradicts rigid theories of dual labor markets. Jobs clearly do matter, but the dynamics of job mobility observed for both white and black men in the Panel Study of Income Dynamics and in other large longitudinal data sets are at odds with the predictions of models based on rigid labor market segmentation.

Instead, there is a fair amount of evidence supporting the human capital model. The patterns of changes in earnings found for white men in the Panel Study were more consistent with the human capital theory. Earnings growth was larger and somewhat more regular for young workers than older ones—facts consistent with the human capital model's prediction that younger workers have the greatest incentives to invest in job skills by undergoing costly on-the-job training. Direct information on the training content of jobs confirmed that younger workers were indeed more likely to be acquiring training. However, it remains an open question whether all training decisions are voluntary and unconstrained, as the human capital model presumes. In addition, the enormous amount of variability in earnings, together with widespread labor market constraints, casts some doubt on human capital theory's assumptions of long-term planning for all classes of workers.

Finally, the evidence presented in this chapter comes mostly from white men. In Chapters 5 and 6 we shall see that the lower earnings of black men and especially of both white and black women cannot be accounted for by differences in acquired job-related skills, and that models explaining the behavior of white men may not apply with equal validity to other, less favored groups in the labor market.

Notes

[1]It could be argued that workers taking seasonal jobs (e.g., in construction) or jobs in volatile industries (e.g., autos) ought to expect a certain amount of unemployment and, indeed, may receive a higher wage rate to compensate for that risk. If such jobs are freely chosen with reliable information about those risks, then subsequent unemployment is not completely involuntary. Unemployment resulting from quitting a job is also somewhat voluntary.

[2]Recall that Panel Study procedures dictate that husbands are the "heads" of husband–wife families. This analysis includes all Panel Study sample individuals who were either heads of their own families (male or female) or wives. Excluded from the analysis are a small number of individuals in this age range who were related in some other way to the household head (e.g., child, brother, or sister).

[3]Fifty weeks of a 40 hour per week job results in a 2,000-hour work year. Time spent on vacation, on sick leave, or unemployed has been subtracted from the reported work hour figures. It should be noted that there is considerable disagreement on the most reliable method for collecting information on work hours. The method used in the Panel Study of recalling the average length of the work week has been shown to be inferior to a time diary approach in which respondents are asked to recall activities during a recent 24-hour period. A comparison of the two approaches shows that the diary method produces a smaller number of work hours reported and a larger change (decline in this case) in the average length of the work week over the past 15 years. See Stafford and Duncan (1980) for a comparison of the two approaches.

[4]For a detailed analysis of these patterns for married women using Panel Study data, see Heckman and Willis (1977).

[5]Findings of small changes in reported work hours should be viewed cautiously, since errors in reporting can produce the appearance of change even if no actual change has taken place. Misreporting an average work week by, say, two hours will produce an apparent annual change of over 100 hours. We should be particularly skeptical about about findings of change in the work hours of married women since it is their husbands who reported those hours, although it is also possible that husbands' reports might understate the true change if they tend to round their responses to a fixed number of hours (e.g., 20 or 40 hours per week).

[6]There is an enormous amount of literature on the relationship between work hours and wage rates, much of it based on cross-sectional data, but some of it based on data from large-scale experiments designed for that specific purpose. We shall not attempt a review of that literature, but rather focus on findings and measures that are unique to the Panel Study. For a particularly careful attempt to estimate the effects of the current U.S. tax system on work hours using Panel Study data, see Hausman (1981).

[7]Work hour adjustments can also be made by changing jobs or taking on second jobs. Job changes are often very costly, however, in terms of lost seniority, pension rights, or costs of relocation. Second jobs often involve search and training costs, as well as additional travel expenses.

[8]This does not mean that overtime work on a salaried job is worthless, however. It may increase one's chances of promotion or of winning a larger salary increase. These rewards are much less certain, though, than an explicit overtime pay rate for workers paid by the hour.

[9]These estimates are taken from Morgan (1979), p. 81. More than three times as many household heads reported working too little than reported working too much for their tastes.

[10]These patterns are by no means consensus estimates of the likely response of work hours to wage rate changes. The availability of longitudinal data has produced a torrent of material on the statistical aspects of estimating labor supply relationships. It will probably be several years before a new consensus is formed on the "best" methods and the "best" estimates. For a review of the econometric issues involved, see Heckman and MacCurdy (1981).

[11]Individuals are "in the labor force" if they are either working or, if not working, are seeking employment. Those who would work if jobs were available but have not been looking are not included in the unemployment counts.

[12]The dashed line in Figure 4.1 shows the fraction of household heads reporting at least

some unemployment in a given calendar year. These fractions are higher than those reported monthly by the Bureau of Labor Statistics because the monthly reports are estimates of unemployment at a point in time rather than during a calendar year.

[13]The importance of education persisted even when differences in occupation and industry were taken into account. It is not merely the types of jobs that the less educated take that lead to greater unemployment; the chronically unemployed can be distinguished by their education even within various kinds of jobs. See Dickinson (1974) for further evidence on the importance of education.

[14]As reported in Corcoran and Hill (1979, pp. 53 and 59), blacks were somewhat more likely to report unemployment in a given year and limited periods of unemployment during the ten-year period. Note that the group being analyzed here—prime-age household heads—does not include individuals from the group of blacks with the highest rates of unemployment—the young.

[15]Training may still be costly even if training and production are joint rather than mutually exclusive activities. If workers compete for jobs with training that lead to higher earnings, then the wages of those jobs will be bid down below the wages paid for similar jobs without such training opportunities.

[16]The analysis presented in this section follows that performed by Dickinson (1974), Duncan (1977), and Corcoran and Datcher (1981) with Panel Study data. As with the labor supply literature, the availability of panel data has produced a flood of econometric work on earnings models. There is no single consensus view on the best methods or the best estimates of the crucial relationships in earnings models. See Heckman (1978) for a recent review of the statistical issues involved.

[17]As noted earlier in this chapter, very few prime-age white men fail to work as many as 500 hours in a given year, so the work hours restriction eliminated very few of them. It was imposed because the principal variable of interest, average hourly earnings, appears to be measured unreliably when work hours are very low. All of the earnings figures have been inflated to 1978 price levels using the Consumer Price Index.

[18]This figure is considerably larger than the 7 percent figure found by Mincer (1974) in his seminal work on human capital earning functions. The following factors add to the explanatory power of education in this analysis: earnings reports are averaged over many years, thus eliminating many of these transitory variations in earnings; the sample is restricted to the more homogeneous group of individuals who were at least 25 years old; and the education–earnings relationship is not constrained to be linear.

[19]One possible counterargument to the interpretation that education's effects are due to increased skills is that schools may merely provide a credential (diploma) that employers use as a screening device. If the composition of jobs in the economy is fairly fixed, then an increase in the educational level of new workers may merely result in an upgrading of the educational requirements of jobs with no actual change in the content of the jobs themselves or in their rate of pay. However, when Duncan and Hoffman (1981a) compared the earnings of workers with more education than their jobs required to those whose educational attainments matched their job requirements, they found that the workers' "surplus" years of education did indeed significantly enhance their earnings. Moreover, workers with *less* education than formally required by their jobs earned less. Education appears to be more than a mere screening credential.

[20]The conclusion that IQ is not an important predictor of economic success has been challenged by findings from a number of studies comparing the economic success of

monozygotic and dizygotic twins. Goldberger (1977), however, has shown that the conclusions of the twins studies are based on a number of very strong and dubious assumptions.

[21]Experience–earnings profiles typically have more of an inverted "U" shape. The relative flatness shown in Figure 4.3 results from the restriction of the sample to workers age 25 years or older in the first year of the ten-year period. Less-experienced workers have much lower earnings than this group. The pattern shown in Figure 4.3 has been adjusted by regression for the effects of all of the variables listed in Table 4.4 as well as region and city size.

[22]Some of these quite explicit predictions about on-the-job training have been supported by analysis of information supplied by respondents in the 1976 interviewing wave about the training content of jobs. Although the amount of training provided by the job was greater for older workers, the chances that an individual was observed to be in a training period were much higher for younger rather than older workers. There was mixed evidence on whether those in training were actually paid less than otherwise similar workers not in training. These analyses are detailed in Duncan and Hoffman (1979, 1980).

[23]Work by Medoff and Abraham (1981) with direct measures of productivity shows that increases in earnings over the life cycle are not matched by the increases in productivity predicted by the human capital model.

[24]The quintiles in Table 4.5 are formed from a ranking of all male workers regardless of race. White workers earn more than workers of other races, so there are slightly fewer than one-fifth of them in the bottom quintiles and more than one-fifth of them in the top.

[25]Schiller (1977) analyzed information reported by employers to the Social Security Administration on the annual income of 75,000 men between 1957 and 1971. Because his sample was so large, he was able to compare the relative earnings change for workers who were all in the same age range. Rather than dividing each age group into wage quintiles, Schiller constructed 20 groups (ventiles). He then compared the ventile position of workers within their own age group in 1957 and 1971, exactly as we did for our quintiles in 1969 and 1978. Schiller also found a large amount of relative income mobility. The correlation between an individual's ventile position in 1956 and in 1971 was extremely low, which means there was very little permanence to an individual's initial income position. On average, individuals moved up or down by more than four ventiles. Schiller concluded (p. 939) "that those labor market models implying high rates of relative earnings mobility have more *ex post* plausibility than various models of stratification."

[26]These survey results are published by the Bureau of Labor Statistics. One reason that median earnings have fallen during the past decade is the unusually large numbers of younger workers now in the labor market, most of whom earn relatively low wages. Their large numbers reflect the baby boom and a very high labor force participation rate for white teenagers.

[27]In fact, there are no definite predictions from the human capital model on the year-to-year variability in earnings. An informal and by no means random survey of proponents of the human capital viewpoint shows that many believe that the paths of individual earnings over time are similar to the cross-sectional results depicted in Figure 4.3, and most grossly underestimate the amount of year-to-year change in earnings.

[28]As with the analysis of ten-year earning mobility, it is probable that errors in measuring earnings generate some of the observed year-to-year income instability. It is impossible to pin down with certainty the likely amount of error; the best we can do is to make some rough estimates and see what difference they make in the results. Hoffman (1977*b*)

did this by examining the sensitivity of the type of results reported in Table 4.6 to the assumption that annual income was underreported in the second of each pair of years by a factor of either 5 percent or 10 percent. With this adjustment, a year-to-year decrease of 5 percent or 10 percent would still be treated as an increase. These adjustments are obviously crude, especially the assumption that errors always cause earnings to be too low (thus creating a spurious decrease in earnings) and never too high (causing an equally spurious increase). In his study of an eight-year period (1967-74), Hoffman found that these adjustments did make a difference in the frequency of year-to-year increases for many individuals. The fraction of individuals with income decreases in no more than one year out of seven increased about five times with the 5 percent adjustment and eight times using the larger error allowance. This still left one-half to two-thirds of the individuals with two or more decreases. Perhaps a reasonable guess as to the true pattern of increases might lie between the no-error calculations in Table 4.6 and these adjusted results. Recognizing measurement error may reduce the variability in earnings streams, but it seems clear that a large amount will still remain.

5

Recent Trends in
the Relative Earnings of Black Men

The volatile economic conditions of the 1960s and 1970s produced both winners and losers, but as a group, black men seem to have been particularly successful in improving their labor market status. Indeed, it is possible to construct a very optimistic consensus view of these trends, as the following indicates.

> Twenty years ago there existed widespread and systematic labor market discrimination against minorities. . . . This discrimination evidenced itself in lower pay for the same work, and (more frequently) less well-paid work for the same objective achievements and abilities. Moreover, this inequality in opportunity was deeply embedded in many important institutions in society; segregated schools at all levels, overt discrimination in employment in the private and public sectors, residential segregation and discrimination in the political sphere, including gerrymandering and outright disenfranchisement in some instances.

> Ten years ago, this landscape had undergone significant change. The federal government had become an active partner of aspiring minority individuals in their efforts to achieve equal rights. The goal of equal opportunity was embodied in the legislation, court rulings and administrative practice. The extent of labor market discrimination, ameliorated by a protracted period of economic expansion, had waned considerably, especially for younger workers. Inequalities in educational and professional opportunities were being rapidly reduced.

> In the past ten years . . . this basic pattern has continued in spite of a generally more sluggish economy. Minority workers entering the labor

force have nearly achieved parity with their nonminority counterparts, both in skills and in earnings. Corporate and government practices toward minority workers, students and citizens have undergone radical change. . . . An emerging elite, professional class of minority workers has developed whose members are, in many instances, better rewarded than their nonminority counterparts. As time goes on and older cohorts are replaced by younger ones, we may expect to see a lasting reversal of the historical patterns of racial economic inequality (Loury and Culp, 1979, pp. 12-13).

Panel Study evidence presented thus far on racial differences in *family* economic status does not justify quite so much optimism about gains in the economic status of blacks. Our data indicate that racial differences in family income were still pervasive enough in the 1970s that the likelihood of either one-year or persistent poverty was far greater for black than for white families. Furthermore, growth in the economic status of initially poor families was lower for blacks than whites during the 1970s, especially for families headed by women.

Yet the evidence for optimism on racial convergence in labor market outcomes for black men seems undeniable.[1] Freeman (1973), for example, used data from several Census Bureau cross-sectional surveys to calculate the median earnings of black and white working men and found that the ratio of black to white median earnings has grown substantially over time, especially since 1965.[2] Typical of these results are that the median earnings of black men were 58 percent of the median earnings of white men in 1959, 67 percent in 1969, and 76 percent in 1978. These comparisons of earnings ratios at several points in time are accompanied by other findings of improvement: Black-to-white earnings ratios for the youngest workers and for the better-educated are considerably higher than the overall averages; black men are moving into the higher-paying occupations previously dominated by white men; and, finally, the general upward trend in the relative earnings of black men seems to have survived the economic downturn and volatility of the early and mid-1970s.

If this optimistic consensus view is accurate it has dramatic implications for policy efforts aimed at improving the relative economic position of black families. To date, policies have either taken the form of ensuring equality of opportunity for blacks or, in the more controversial affirmative action programs, have attempted to redress the effects of past discrimination by favoring qualified blacks over equally qualified whites. If it is true that young black and white men now begin their careers on equal footing, then the more controversial programs might no longer be necessary, particularly in view of the costs of the ill will they have generated.[3] However, there are a number of important empirical questions to be considered in evaluating the relative level and recent change in the economic status of black men—questions that can best be addressed with the rich longitudinal information available in the Panel Study.

A first question is whether comparisons from cross-sectional data accurately reflect the longer-term relative labor market positions of black and white men. When the period over which earnings are measured is extended beyond one year we find that the wage affluence of black men is more temporary than it is for white men, while wage poverty is more permanent. Fewer than 2 percent of black (versus 11 percent of white) working men were persistently in the top fifth of the wage distribution in the late 1970s, although this fraction for blacks was higher than it was in the late 1960s. Black men were twice as likely as white men to be persistently in the bottom fifth of the wage distribution. These findings cast doubt on assertions that a sizable and permanent black upper-middle class has been established.

A second set of questions involves the structure of earnings differences that are observed for black and white men in the 1970s. Can these differences be attributed to measurable differences in family background and schooling, implying that current labor market discrimination is unimportant? If family background differences are sizable, do they imply that current discrepancies in family economic status will handicap future generations of black workers? Here we find that nearly half of the earnings differences between black and white working men can be attributed to their two-year difference in completed schooling. But differences in schooling and early labor market attainment, in turn, can be attributed in part to differences in the economic position of black and white families and in part to differences in the neighborhoods in which black and white children are raised. Whether current patterns of residential segregation are voluntary or not, they do appear to exert an independent effect on the attainments of young black and white men that could slow down or even halt improvements in the status of future generations of black workers.

In addition to questions about the relative level of attainment for blacks are questions about recent trends in attainment. Do the earnings of individual black and white working men show the same growth patterns as the aggregate ratios? The answer is clearly negative, according to Panel Study information. Among working men already in the labor force, the wages of blacks do not appear to be growing much faster than the wages of whites; among young working men, wage growth appears higher for whites than blacks. The improvement in median earnings ratios is due, in large part, to the fact that the starting pay rates of new black working men have moved closer to white pay rates.

A final question is whether the patterns of change are consistent with prevailing explanations of black-white wage differentials. Here we find little evidence that recent improvements in the economic status of black working men can be traced to improvements in such measured characteristics as education. Blacks are acquiring more education now than before, but so are whites. The improved relative earnings may well be due to antidiscrimination efforts by the government, but if so, the changes are concentrated at the beginning of work careers and not among workers already in the labor force.

The Nature of Earnings "Poverty" and "Affluence"

Changes in the labor market position of blacks are usually measured by year-to-year changes in average hourly or annual earnings. It is also important to monitor trends in longer-term status. Concepts of an "elite" income class or of a class that is permanently earnings-poor imply a status that persists beyond a single year. Although cross-sectional data on occupational position do indicate a longer-term status, multiple observations on the earnings of individual black and white working men are much more direct measures of longer-term position. Because cross-sectional data sets are restricted to a single point in time (and survey reports of income received more than a year ago are not very reliable) they cannot provide the needed information. In contrast, longitudinal data such as those from the Panel Study can be used for such purposes.

The following analysis (Duncan and Hoffman, 1981b) is based on 12 years of information (1967–1978) on individual earnings. To facilitate an understanding of trends in relative earnings over the 12 years, we treat the 12 years of information as three 4-year panels for the time periods 1967–70, 1971–74, and 1975–78. Included in the analysis for each of the three 4-year periods are those male household heads who were aged 25 to 54 in the first year of a given period (i.e., in 1967, 1971, and 1975), and who worked at least 500 hours in each year of the 4-year observation period.[4]

We first note that the "snapshot" pictures of improvement in the relative economic status of blacks for these three time periods are quite similar to those found by other researchers using other sources of data. The ratios of the median black male worker's wages to the median white male worker's wages were .65 for 1967, .70 for 1971, and .76 for 1975. These figures change little when wages are averaged over each of the four-year periods, indicating that the one-year earnings position of black and white working men in the middle of the wage distribution are representative of the multi-year average status of those in the middle.[5] More will be said about comparisons of "average" working men later on. Turning our attention from the middle of the earnings distribution, we examine both the top and bottom earnings positions, using the concepts of earnings "affluence" and earnings "poverty." To define these concepts, we take each year separately and rank all of these men into one of five quintiles according to their hourly wage rate. The wage rates separating the top and the bottom fifths (quintiles) of these workers from the rest are found for each of the 12 years.[6] In 1978, for example, one-fifth of these men earned less than $5.46 per hour, while one-fifth earned more than $11.58 per hour. Workers with hourly earnings high enough to place them in the top 20 percent of the male earnings distribution are defined as "earnings affluent" in that year, while those in the bottom fifth are "earnings poor." Information gathered over the three 4-year periods can be used to measure "occasional" and "persistent" earnings affluence and poverty: "Occasional" is defined as being in the top or bottom fifth of the earnings distribution in *at least* one of the four years, and "persistent" is defined as being in the top or bottom fifth in *every* one of the four years.

Table 5.1 shows the proportion of black and white working men who were occasionally or persistently in the top or bottom fifth of the wage distribution in each of the three 4-year periods.[7] Consider first the figures for the final 4-year period, 1975-1978, shown in the last two columns of Table 5.1. About one in six black men (15.5 percent) and twice as many white men (32.5 percent) earned enough to place them in the top fifth of the earnings distribution in at least one of the four years. Wage affluence is not very permanent, however, especially for blacks. Fewer than 2 of every 100 black working men (1.7 percent) in this representative sample earned enough to be persistently affluent. The incidence of persistent earnings affluence for white men was 11.4 percent—more than six times as great as for blacks. So while the earnings of the average black working man inch closer to those of the average white working man, a black's chances of securing a longer-term position in the upper end of the earnings distribution was very small and several times less than the comparable chances for a white working man.

Table 5.1

OCCASIONAL AND PERSISTENT EARNINGS AFFLUENCE AND POVERTY FOR
BLACK AND WHITE MEN

| | Time Period | | | | | |
| | 1967–1970 | | 1971–1974 | | 1975–1978 | |
	Black Men	White Men	Black Men	White Men	Black Men	White Men
Earnings Affluence:						
Percent ever in top fifth of the hourly earnings distribution	6.6%	33.9%	10.4%	32.8%	15.5%	32.5%
Percent always in top fifth of the hourly earnings distribution	0.0	11.7	0.3	13.2	1.7	11.4
Earnings Poverty:						
Percent ever in bottom fifth of the hourly earnings distribution	66.0	28.9	56.5	31.4	45.7	31.6
Percent always in bottom fifth of the hourly earnings distribution	28.3	8.9	25.4	6.4	19.8	8.0

Table reads: "Only 6.6% of all black men, and 33.9% of white men, had hourly earnings high enough to place them in the top fifth of the wage distribution in at least one of the four years between 1967 and 1970; none of the black men, and 11.7% of the white men, placed in the top fifth in all four of those years."

As slim as the chances of persistent wage affluence are for a black, they seem to have improved over the 12-year period. During the 1971–74 interval, only 0.3 percent of black men were persistently affluent, and in the 1967–70 period, not a single one of the 293 black men in the sample earned enough in each of the four years to warrant that designation. A similar improvement can also be seen in the chances of occasional earnings affluence. Although black men were only half as likely as white men to have high earnings in at least one of the years between 1975 and 1978, eight years earlier (in the 1967–70 period) black men were less than one-fifth as likely as white men to have at least one year of high earnings.

Wage poverty, on the other hand, was much more common among black men. Occasional wage poverty was experienced by nearly two-thirds of black working men in the first 4-year period (1967–70) and still by nearly half of black working men in the final period (1971–74). In comparison, occasional wage poverty was experienced by less than one-third of white working men in each of the three periods. Black men's chances of persistent wage poverty declined somewhat over the 12 years, but were still about two and a half times as high as for white men.

In sum, changes in the earnings of the median or average black and white working man indicate much greater trends toward equality than do changes in the earnings of those at the upper and lower quintiles of the earnings distribution. Despite considerable improvements during the late 1960s and 1970s, persistent wage affluence in the late 1970s remained rare among black working men and was six times more likely among white working men. Persistent earnings poverty as we have defined it, on the other hand, characterized close to 20 percent of all black working men, compared to only 8 percent of all white working men.

Explaining the Differences

That the ratio of black to white median earnings has increased from three-fifths to three-quarters in the past two decades raises questions about its level and trend. Why aren't black men's earnings *equal* to those of whites; that is, why aren't these ratios close to or in excess of 1.0? Why have they risen so markedly? There is considerable disagreement over the answers to both of these questions, a disagreement ultimately concerning the nature, extent, and even existence of labor market discrimination and the policies that have been designed to combat it. An understanding of the controversy requires a brief explanation of the theories of discrimination.

Theories of Discrimination

The theory of discrimination most popular among economists was developed by Becker (1957).[8] It views discrimination as an *individual* preference of employers who operate in a reasonably competitive economic environment.[9] A discriminatory employer is defined as one who is willing to hire a white worker over an equally productive black even if a higher wage is required to hire the white. Indeed, the wage premium can be viewed as a measure of the discriminatory preference.

One result of these forms of discrimination is that blacks are paid less than whites for the same skills. Viewed in a dynamic context, however, these forms of discrimination cannot persist indefinitely. Since discriminatory employers must pay a wage premium to hire a white over an equally qualified black worker, their work force is either higher-paid or less productive than the work force of nondiscriminatory employers. In a competitive economic environment, nondiscriminatory employers should incur lower costs, earn higher profits, expand, and either drive the discriminatory employers out of business or force them to abandon their discriminatory behavior.[10]

The policy implications that follow from this view are decidedly *laissez faire*. The dynamic operation of a competitive economy should reduce and eventually eliminate discrimination. Policies that intervene in decisions regarding hiring and promotion policies of firms will, if anything, hurt rather than help by burdening employers with unnecessary costs and creating incentives for them to evade the policies.

There are several alternative explanations of discrimination, most of them based on institutional labor market constraints rather than individual employers. According to these explanations, earnings are determined largely by the particular labor markets in which individuals work rather than by the skills (human capital) they possess.

Labor market discrimination is a key element in the dual labor market theory discussed in Chapter 4. According to this theory the labor market consists of two sectors, primary and secondary. Jobs in the primary sector provide stable employment, good wages, and, more important, an opportunity to learn new skills and eventually obtain even better jobs. Blue-collar jobs in unionized employment or within the more capital-intensive industries and white-collar jobs within large organizations are usually thought· to be examples of these primary sector jobs. In contrast, the secondary sector jobs such as dishwashing, casual labor, and some nonunionized blue-collar work provide lower wages, unstable employment, and no real opportunity to learn new skills. Proponents of this explanation argue that one manifestation of discrimination is to deny black workers access to the better jobs in the primary labor market and to relegate them to the dead-end jobs in the secondary labor market.[11] Moreover, those blacks who can find primary sector employment may face discrimination in promotions. The sources and mechanisms of discrimination itself and their relationship to a firm's objectives are not discussed carefully by proponents of this model. Instead, the institutional view assumes the existence of discrimination and the presence of labor markets that are not very competitive, concluding that interventionist policies are effective ways of attacking the problem.

Still other models take a Marxist perspective, viewing labor market discrimination as a means by which those in the capitalist class attempt to maintain and enhance their privileged class position. In this view, a capitalist policy would encourage discriminatory policies and attitudes within the work force as a way to divide workers, reducing the likelihood that workers will perceive their common interests and organize themselves into a powerful bargaining or, in the extreme, revolutionary force. The Marxist model implies that capitalists have more to gain than they lose by discrimination, in contrast to the predictions of the competitive, individual-based preference explanations, and thus also suggests the sources of labor market discrimination, as the institutional labor market explanation does not.

Although there are radical differences in the assumptions and predictions of these various theories of discrimination, it is surprisingly difficult to distinguish between them empirically. Survey evidence on reported motives for behavior is often unreliable in the best of circumstances, and when the behavior under study is as controversial and threatening as personnel policies regarding minority workers, survey responses are completely untrustworthy. The approach taken in most empirical studies of discrimination and in this chapter as well is based on survey data on the earnings and other characteristics of a representative sample of black and white working men.

Wage Differentials and Discrimination

The relationship between the earnings differences between black and white working men and the extent of discrimination is, at best, indirect. Earnings differences between groups may arise for reasons unrelated to labor market discrimination. In a market economy, wages are related to productivity and hence to individual skills. Many skills, most notably those learned in school, are acquired prior to entry into the labor market. Decisions about the acquisition of these skills are often made jointly by a child and his or her parents and may be influenced by discrimination in housing, credit, and labor markets faced by the parents when the child was growing up. It becomes important, then, to understand the ways in which family background factors affect the attainment of blacks and whites. Earlier research (Duncan, 1969) found that the link between family background and attainment was considerably weaker for black men than white men, suggesting that improvements in the current economic status of black working men would not be translated readily into improvements in attainment for the next generation of black workers. More recent research appears to indicate that the link between background and attainment for black men is now quite similar to that of white men.[12]

Although race-related differences in skills acquired prior to entry into the labor market can be expected to lead to wage differences, these differences cannot be attributed to *current* labor market discrimination. In contrast, other skills, most notably those received through on-the-job training, are obtained in the current labor market. Differences in the amount of on-the-job training may result from discriminatory access to training opportunities, or they may result from voluntary career decisions made by individual workers.

Inferring discrimination from wage differentials is a tricky business. It is not proper to attribute all of the earnings gap to current labor market discrimination, since some of the differences may be due to skills acquired prior to entry into the labor market. For example, both the quality and quantity of formal schooling has been lower for blacks than whites (Welch, 1973). Similarly, the differential that remains after the effects of skill differences have been removed cannot properly be considered an estimate of discrimination, since some of the skill differences themselves may have resulted from past labor market discrimination, and the relevant skill factors may not all have been measured.[13] An estimate of wage differences associated with skill differences is a valuable first step, however, since the remaining wage differences are a rough upper bound estimate of the possible magnitude of current labor market discrimination.

When we used a host of characteristics related to productivity to explain the $1.77 gap in earnings that existed between black and white men in 1975, we found (Corcoran and Duncan, 1978) that about 40 percent of the gap could be explained by a nearly two-year difference in the educational attainment of the two groups.[14] Black men, on average, had completed 11.0 years of education; white men had finished 12.9 years. Additional years of schooling raised the earnings of blacks and whites by similar amounts. When this earnings increment was used to assess the economic impact of the schooling difference, it was found that two-fifths of the wage gap could be accounted for by the schooling difference. In the case of education, the labor market appears to be operating efficiently in the sense that it gives similar pay increments to those with higher levels of education, regardless of race. Although this schooling difference may have been caused by discriminatory policies regarding access to or financial incentives towards the acquisition of more education, the earnings differential that arises from the two-year average difference in educational level is not due to current labor market discrimination.

Effects of Family Background on Schooling and Early Career Attainment

That racial differences in schooling account for two-fifths of the earnings differences between black and white working men points to the importance of understanding how family background factors affect the early attainments of black and white workers. The nature of these background effects has important implications for the desirability of affirmative action programs. Opponents of these programs argue that in redressing past violations of the rights of minorities, affirmative action programs subvert the rights of nonminority workers. Some proponents have pointed to evidence that not only do blacks come from less advantaged backgrounds than whites but also that the link between background and attainment for blacks is weaker than for whites. As a result, they argue, merely equalizing the educational and employment opportunities of the current generation of workers will not produce equal outcomes within a reasonable period of time.

A more sophisticated argument along these lines is developed by Loury (1976), who considers not only the intergenerational dynamics of family income but also the consequences of racial segregation in housing. These racial patterns in housing affect the neighborhood schools, leading to differences in educational quality, in the backgrounds and aspirations of the student body, and perhaps in access to job information and influence networks. If neighborhoods affect an individual's economic status independent of his or her family, it is possible to show, at least in theory, that these neighborhood effects will prevent the equalization of opportunities from having the desired result of equalizing attainment.

Datcher (1982) examined the effects of family background and neighborhood quality on the attainment of black and white working men, using the group of young men in the Panel Study sample who were living with their parents in the early years of the study but subsequently split off to form their own households. For this group, family background measures such as parental schooling and income level are reported by parents rather than recalled by the children, so they are likely to be measured fairly precisely. In addition to the set of family background measures, consideration was given to measures of the *community* of origin—specifically, its average income level and its racial composition.[15] She found substantial effects of background variables on the educational attainment and earnings of the young black men, with the community measures accounting for about one-fourth of the total background effect. For white men, the parental measures had even larger effects than they did for black men, while the community effects were not as consistently important.[16] She found that raising the quality of the backgrounds of blacks to the levels of whites would have increased black educational attainment by more than a half year and black earnings by over 25 percent (Datcher, 1982, p. 39). Differences in community quality made up about one-quarter of this effect.

Earnings Over the Life Cycle

In addition to the schooling differences between blacks and whites, additional years of labor market experience of the 1975 sample appeared to add much more to the earnings of white than to those of black working men. When viewed as a point-in-time cross section, the relationship between years of labor market experience and earnings for the black and white men in the Panel Study sample mirrors the pattern found by others using different sets of cross-sectional data. As Figure 5.1 shows, the earnings gap between white and black working men in the Panel Study is clearly much larger for those with 20 to 40 years of work experience than for those just starting out.[17] These patterns, based on working men of different ages at a point in time, have been used to predict the future earnings paths of young male workers as they acquire additional years of work experience. Such cross-sectional data appear to indicate that black working men encounter increasing discrimination as they grow older. One economist who studied the question by using data of this sort concluded that "the whole notion of a career with steady advancement is relevant only for white males" (Hall, 1973, p. 393).

The conclusion that discrimination increases over the life cycle has been challenged because the findings of divergent earnings paths are based on cross-sectional information about *different* individuals of *different* ages rather than the *same* individuals as they aged. In particular, some speculate that the larger earnings gap for more experienced workers might be due either to large differences between blacks and whites in the quality of education, especially for older southern blacks, or to the lingering effects of the more severe labor market discrimination that older blacks faced when they first looked for jobs.[18] For example, a cross-sectional sample of people aged 20–60 years in 1975 would inevitably reflect birth years from 1915–1955, and years of entry into the labor market from about 1930 to 1975. Thus the effects of the different social and economic milieus prevalent at various stages of the individuals' life

Figure 5.1

HOURLY EARNINGS BY YEARS OF EXPERIENCE IN 1975

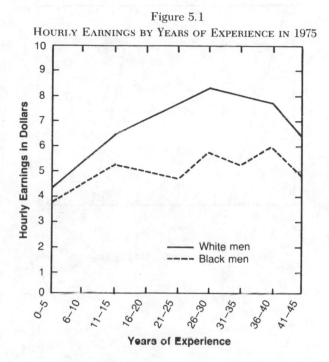

cycle produce "vintage effects"— the unmeasured differences between older and younger workers—rather than any inherent tendency toward increasing discrimination over the life cycle.

An obvious way to resolve these questions about life-cycle earnings patterns is by using longitudinal data on the earnings of the same individuals over time, as in the Panel Study. By comparing rates of earnings growth for black and white working men, one can see to what extent they differ and to what extent earnings diverge over the life cycle. A study of this kind was conducted by Hoffman (1979), using information on earnings between 1967 and 1974 for white and black male workers who were in their twenties and thirties in 1967. He found that elements of both the "increasing discrimination with age" and the "vintage effects" explanations are correct. Figure 5.2 summarizes the findings for the two groups of working men.[19]

For the younger male workers, born between 1938 and 1947, racial earnings differences did tend to increase with each additional year of work experience. Consider, for example, what happened between 1967

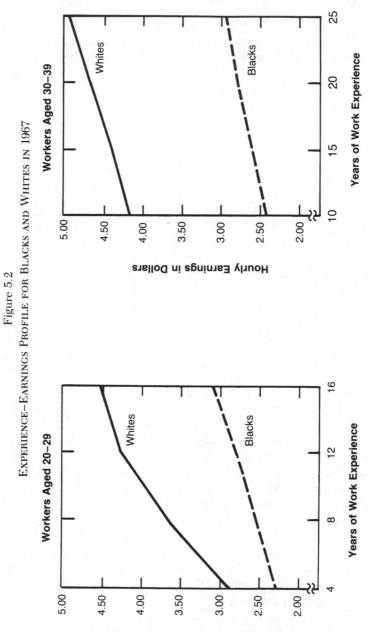

Figure 5.2

EXPERIENCE–EARNINGS PROFILE FOR BLACKS AND WHITES IN 1967

and 1974 to the earnings of those who had been working for six years as of 1967. In 1967, the average earnings of the white male workers in this group were about $3.30 per hour, while the black male workers' earnings were about $2.40 per hour—some 72 percent of the average earnings for whites. Over the next eight years, however, the earnings of the whites grew almost twice as rapidly as those of the blacks. By 1974, the average earnings of the white male workers had risen by almost a dollar an hour (in real terms, adjusted for inflation), while the earnings of the black male workers grew by only about forty-five cents. As a result, the average black man's earnings had fallen to only about 67 percent of the average white man's earnings, compared with 72 percent in 1967. The differential growth in earnings from 1967 to 1974 was less dramatic for those who had had more years of work experience in 1967, but throughout this age group the earnings of white men grew more rapidly than those of blacks.

For the working men in their thirties, born between 1928 and 1937, Figure 5.2 tells quite a different story. Since the earnings growth for both the black and white men was almost identical, there was no indication that the black workers faced *increasing* discrimination. Instead they faced a consistently larger earnings gap: black men in this age group earned only about 60 percent as much as white men.

It appears, then, that by the time they are in their thirties, both black and white working men experience roughly equal wage growth, but at an earlier stage, while still in their twenties, white men's jobs provide considerably higher wage growth than do the jobs of black men. Some supporting evidence for this conclusion comes from questions asked about on-the-job training during the 1976 interview.[20] All respondents were asked about the training content of their jobs, and it was possible to compare reports of job tenure and training time to see how many of the workers were still engaged in on-the-job training. Presumably those who were still in training would be more likely to enjoy future earnings growth. Note that being in training could result either from holding a job that provides a great deal of training or from promotions or other job changes into new positions with training.

Table 5.2 shows the proportion of black and white working men of different ages who were still engaged in training. Dramatic differences show up for the youngest groups of working men. More than one-third of white working men in their twenties or early thirties were still in their training periods compared to only about one-tenth of the corresponding black working men. The racial gap in training is smaller for the

Table 5.2

PROPORTION OF WORKING MEN STILL IN TRAINING ON THEIR CURRENT JOBS,
BY RACE AND AGE

Age	White Men	Black Men
Less than 25 years	35.3%	7.4%
25 to 34 years	34.9	10.3
35 to 44 years	23.0	7.3
45 to 54 years	17.6	11.3
55 to 64 years	13.5	7.9
All	25.8%	9.1%
Number of observations	2,250	895

Table reads: "More than one-third (35.3%) of white men under the age of 25 were still in the training periods of their current jobs. . . ."
Source: Duncan and Hoffman (1978), p. 145.

older groups of workers. Thus if wage growth is dependent upon training opportunities, then these training differences are consistent with the largest earnings growth rate differentials found for the youngest workers.[21]

This chapter opened with a review of evidence that the racial earnings gap was growing smaller over time. On the face of it, the evidence presented in this section on the lower or, at best, equal growth rates for black relative to white male workers appears to contradict the unmistakable *increase* in the black/white earnings ratio. If the earnings of blacks and whites grow at the same percentage rate, then the black/white earnings ratio ought to remain fixed.[22] If growth rates favor white men, then the ratio ought to decline. And yet we observed that the ratio has *increased* over time. In the next section, we will reconcile this apparent contradiction.

Recent Trends in Relative Earnings

The upward trend in the relative earnings of black men, observed by many in data from the Census Bureau, shows up in the Panel Study data as well. To show this, we follow a strategy similar to that used in our investigation of earnings affluence and poverty, treating 12 years of information between 1967 and 1978 as three 4-year panels for the time periods 1967–70, 1971–74, and 1975–78, respectively. As before, the sample for each 4-year panel is restricted to those male household heads who were age 25 to 54 in the first year of each period (1967, 1971, 1975)

Table 5.3

BLACK-TO-WHITE WAGE RATIOS FOR VARIOUS YEARS
(Three Separate Cohorts of 25- to 54-Year-Old Male Household Heads)

Year	Black-to-White Wage Ratio	
	For All Workers (Age 25 to 54)	For Young Workers Only (Age 25 to 34)
1967–70 Average	65%	72%
1967	64	75
1968	66	73
1969	64	70
1970	65	70
1971–74 Average	70	78
1971	71	81
1972	70	81
1973	70	78
1974	69	73
1975–78 Average	76	80
1975	75	81
1976	76	80
1977	77	80
1978	76	81

Table reads: "Over the 4-year period 1967–70, wages earned by black working men age 25–54 averaged 65% of the wages earned by white working men age 25–54; for young working men (age 25–34) only, the black-to-white wage ratio was 72%."

and who worked at least 500 hours in each year of that period. Thus the composition of three successive samples changes as some of those workers pass beyond the 54-year age limit and are excluded from the subsequent sample period and others reach the age of 25 and become eligible for the first time.[23]

Table 5.3 shows black/white hourly earnings ratios when earnings are averaged over the 4-year periods as well as for the individual years within each of the 4-year periods. Separate results are also presented for the subset of working men who were between the ages of 25 and 34 in 1967, 1971, and 1975. The improvement in average wage ratios corresponds to findings from other data sources. For these representative samples of working 25- to 54-year-olds, the ratio of average wage rates of black and white male workers rose from about 65 percent in 1967–70 to almost 70 percent in 1971–74 to 76 percent in 1975–78. For the younger groups of working men, the wage rate ratio rose from 72 percent to 80 percent.

The path of earnings ratios *within* each of the 4-year periods shows a strikingly different pattern, especially for the 25- to 34-year-old working men. Rather than approximating the trend of steady increases, ratios within each of the 4-year periods are generally constant or even slightly falling. For example, although average wage ratios for the two sets of 25- to 54-year-olds rose from 65 to 70 percent from 1967–70 to 1971–74, the trend within the first 4-year period showed only a 1 percent increase. Similar trends also occurred in the two subsequent periods: while aggregate ratios continued to rise, the within-period ratio actually fell from 1971 to 1974 and rose only slightly from 1975 to 1978. Even among young male workers where wage convergence has been most highly publicized, the same conflicting trends appear between and within the cohorts. Consistent with the evidence discussed earlier that growth rates were lower for young black than for young white men, the wage ratio for the younger workers fell five percentage points from 1967 to 1970. Within-cohort ratios also fell sharply over the 1971–74 period and were stable for the last four years.

The numbers presented in Table 5.3 provide a way to reconcile the findings of improvement over time in earnings ratios by race with the findings of constancy or even decline in the earnings ratios within each period. The key is that the first type of statistic—comparisons of cross sections of working men who are in a given age range at two points in time—involves comparing a changing group of workers. That is, the comparison will measure changes experienced by a smaller, *continuing* group of working men who remain within the age range for the period in question, but will also measure any changes produced as a result of the *departure* of an older group that is no longer within the specified age range by the second point in time and the *arrival* of a younger group that has entered this age range. Earnings ratios for the continuing group may be declining, but the aggregate ratios may still increase if the relative earnings position of the younger entering group is sufficiently favorable or if the position of the departing older group is sufficiently unfavorable relative to the continuing group.[24] Aggregate ratios, in other words, are weighted averages of continuing, departing, and entering groups, and it is important to recognize this and treat each group separately.

Duncan and Hoffman (1983) calculated the relative importance of the entering, continuing, and departing cohorts of working men for the changes in the earnings between the 1967–70 and the 1975–78 samples of working men shown in Table 5.3. They found that about three-fifths of the improvement was due to higher earnings ratios for the entering group of workers, only about one-third was due to an improvement in the relative earnings of blacks in the continuing group, and less than one-tenth was due to the departing group of workers. This relative importance of the entering group of workers vis-a-vis the continuing group casts a different light on the most common interpretation of the causes of improvement.

One obvious explanation for improvement is governmental action—passage of the 1964 Civil Rights Act and the cumulative impact of the Equal Employment Opportunity Commission. Freeman has documented the striking change in the path of black/white earnings that occurred around 1964, from a very slight trend prior to 1964 to a sharp, upward trend afterward.

The analysis of trends over the 12-year period with Panel Study data shows that the rising ratios were due more to the favorable position of black men just entering the labor force than to any improvement in the position of black men already in the labor market. Thus, what effects those policies may have had appeared to be concentrated at the beginning of the work-life cycle, and were not felt so much during the careers of those already in the labor force. It is, of course, possible that the improved position of young black working men is due to a relative improvement in their skills and not to any policy effects. But this does not seem to have been the case. Black working men in the entering cohort were better educated than older black working men, but so were young white working men relative to older whites. The *net* contribution of the relative increase in black educational attainment was quite small. None of the other measured characteristics were able to account for the improved position of the younger black men. It may be due to such unmeasured characteristics as differences in school quality, which were noted by Welch (1973) for earlier periods. This seems unlikely during the seventies, however, especially in the secondary schools. Although government policies may have led to a favorable position for black labor market entrants, the evidence supporting this conclusion is only indirect.

Summary and Implications

That the relative labor market position of the average black working man has improved over the past two decades is undeniable. But an examination of the patterns of relative earnings with the longitudinal information from the Panel Study casts a different light on some of these findings and implications.

First and foremost is the fact that the heavily documented rising ratio

of median earnings of black and white working men does not mean that
the relative economic position of most black working men has improved.
The popular findings are based on comparisons of two cross sections of
workers in a given age range and involve a changing set of individuals.
We found that more than half of the improvement between the late
1960s and late 1970s in the relative wages of black working men could
be attributed to the high relative earnings of the newly entering group
of youngest men in the late 1970s. The improvement for black men
working during the entire time was much less than the rising ratios
would indicate. Indeed, there was some evidence that young black men
in their twenties actually had lower wage growth than their white counterparts and, consequently, that younger black men may actually lose
ground relative to white men in the initial years of their careers. This
picture was supported by some evidence of a substantial gap between
young black and white men in the amount of on-the-job training they
were receiving.

Although training differences may erode the subsequent economic
position of blacks, it does appear that the starting position of young black
men is much closer to that of young white men than it used to be. How
can this improvement be explained? Here the Panel Study evidence
casts doubt on explanations that attribute this to the improved skills of
black working men. Young black men have indeed had more education
than older black men, but so have young white men relative to older
white men. The *relative* improvement in the measured skills of young
black working men is too small to be an important factor in their improved economic status. It is tempting to attribute the gains to policy
efforts undertaken on behalf of blacks since the mid-1960s, but we have
no direct evidence to support that contention.

A second important point concerns the usefulness of wage ratios
themselves as indicators of the relative status of black working men.
Toward the end of the 1970s the average black working man earned
about three-quarters as much as his white counterpart. Comparisons
such as these of the wage levels of black and white working men in the
middle of the wage distribution in a single year do not reflect the relative position of blacks at the high and low ends of the distribution, nor
do they indicate the persistence of that position. We found that very few
black men were persistently in the top end of the earnings distribution,
indicating that reports of a substantial emerging "black elite" may be
exaggerated. Although the fraction of black men persistently in the top
fifth of the wage distribution has increased over the past dozen years,

the chance of persistent wage affluence in the late 1970s for white men was still six times as high as for black men. Persistent wage poverty, on the other hand, characterized about twice as many black as white working men.

Expectations about the future position of blacks and the development of policies most likely to improve it need to be based on a thorough understanding of the processes that determine the economic status of blacks and whites. In Chapter 4 we saw that the large fluctuations in earnings and the substantial movement of black working men between different kinds of jobs cast serious doubt on models of the labor market that postulate impenetrable boundaries between sectors. Black men are more heavily concentrated into lower-paying, lower-skill jobs, but they are not locked into them permanently. By the same token, those black men currently holding higher-paying jobs cannot expect their favored positions to be permanent.

Part of the reason that black men are found in lower-skill jobs is that they bring fewer skills to the labor market when they begin their careers. The two-year schooling disadvantage of black working men accounted for nearly half of their earnings deficit. Even in the absence of discrimination, an efficient labor market cannot be expected to ignore these schooling differences when allocating workers to jobs. An obvious implication is that earnings differences will not disappear as long as black and white workers bring different levels of skill to the labor market.

The task of equalizing the average labor market position of black and white men is likely to be a difficult one. The family and community environments of blacks and whites differ markedly, and both environments play an important role in schooling and early career decisions. We have seen that the family economic position of blacks is much worse than that of whites, and the discrepancy does not appear to have become smaller in the past few years. Recent improvements in the labor market position of black men ought to improve the family environment of the next generation of black workers, but the weakness of the link between family background and attainment ensures that this process will be a slow one. Evidence that early attainment is affected by the composition and quality of neighborhoods in which blacks and whites are raised is especially troublesome. It raises the likelihood that if patterns of residential segregation persist, then gains in black men's earnings and family income may never equalize the economic status of future generations of black and white working men. Policies aimed directly at residential desegregation are one option, although resistance to them has been strong. Alternative policies to ensure equal opportunity for education and jobs can be developed, but most would require that substantial resources be allocated to compensate for the effects of disadvantaged backgrounds.

Notes

[1]See, in particular, the studies by Freeman (1973, 1978), Welch (1978), Smith and Welch (1977), and Haworth, et al. (1975).

[2]The median black working man is in the middle of a ranking of all black working men by earnings—half of all black working men earn more than he does, half less. The median white working man is similarly defined.

[3]A comprehensive discussion of the issues surrounding these policies would take us far afield. See Loury (1981) for a discussion of these policies and evidence that bears upon them.

[4]Note that some of the older working men in the 1967–70 period will not meet the age restriction for the 1971–74 period, and older working men in the 1971–74 period will not be part of the 1975–78 period analysis. By the same token, new young male workers will be brought into analysis in the second and third periods. Restricting the sample to individual men who worked at least 500 hours in each of the four years also excludes those with prolonged unemployment or nonparticipation due to illness, discouragement, or other reasons. The effects of these exclusions are not large, however. For white men, almost 6 percent of the male household heads in the specified age range were excluded during the 1967–1970 period compared to 13.5 percent of black male household heads. In the 1975–1978 period, these exclusions affected 9.6 percent of the white and 15.6 percent of the black male household heads. In both time periods and for both races, those excluded were less educated, on average, and less urbanized than those included.

[5]This does not necessarily mean that earnings are quite stable from one year to the next, however. In fact, individual earnings are quite volatile, but the fluctuations average out.

[6]This procedure is analogous to those followed in Chapters 1 and 4, where families and workers were ranked according to their income level and divided into quintiles, or five equal groups. Here we are concerned only with the top and bottom quintiles and not with the middle three.

[7]The descriptive results presented in this section are consistent with a much more sophisticated analysis of the persistence of wage poverty conducted on Panel Study data by Lillard and Willis (1978) and a comparable study of the persistence of wage affluence conducted by Datcher (forthcoming).

[8]For a general discussion of theories of discrimination, see Pascal (1972), especially the chapters by Arrow; or see Masters (1975).

[9]Becker (1957) also develops models of discrimination based on the preferences of employers and customers.

[10]This theory does not consider the effect of prolonged discrimination on the acquisition of market skills, however, and implicitly assumes that the elimination of discriminatory preferences immediately ends the consequences of discrimination.

[11]These arguments are detailed in Doeringer and Piore (1971). Less extreme versions

of the theory view the process of allocating good jobs to workers as following a queue, with blacks positioned toward the end of the queue. If enough jobs become available, then blacks will eventually get them.

[12]See, for example, Featherman and Hauser (1976) and Freeman (1978).

[13]See Butler (1982) for a more formal discussion of these problems.

[14]These men were between the ages of 25 and 64, were heads of their own households, and had worked at least 500 hours during 1975. The average hourly earnings of white and black men were $6.67 and $4.90, respectively. The complete set of explanatory variables is listed in Chapter 6, Table 6.1.

[15]The community data were taken from the 1970 Census Fifth Count for Zip Codes and matched to the sample respondents living in Standard Metropolitan Statistical Areas by their five-digit zip code number. The information was not available for those in 1968 families who lived outside of SMSA's, and they were not included in the analysis.

[16]The finding that the effects of background on attainment were more important for white than for black men appears to contradict recent work cited earlier that shows virtual racial equality in these effects. Panel Study information show some, but by no means complete, convergence in effects of background. Furthermore, a reexamination of the earlier evidence on convergence raises some doubts about its strength (see Datcher, 1981).

[17]Figure 5.1 is analogous to Figure 4.4 (Chapter 4), which was based on the ten-year average earnings of white men. Figure 5.1 is based on one-year (1975) earnings of black and white men.

[18]Finis Welch and James P. Smith are the most prolific proponents of this explanation. See Smith and Welch (1977) and Welch (1978).

[19]The heights of the lines in Figure 5.1 and Figure 5.2 do not correspond since they use different base years to adjust for inflation. The wage levels in Figure 5.1 are expressed in 1975 dollars. The levels in Figure 5.2 are in 1967 dollars.

[20]Additional supporting evidence from two other longitudinal data sets is given in Lazear (1979).

[21]The results are not completely consistent with findings of equal growth rates for older working men, since training differences continue to favor the older white men.

[22]Suppose that the average black wage is $6 per hour and the average white wage is $8 per hour. The wage ratio is 6/8 = .75. If wages of both groups grow by ten percent, then the new averages will be $6.60 and $8.80, but the ratio will still be .75.

[23]It is also possible that the composition of the group of working men meeting the age requirements in 1967, 1971, and 1975 will change. Some of them may have dropped out of the labor force through death, disability, or discouragement. Others may have entered the labor force during this time as well.

[24]A simple example may help to explain this. Suppose we compare the earnings of black and white working men between the ages of 30 and 50 years in 1970 and 1980. Suppose further that all black working men in their thirties and forties earn $5 and $7 per hour, respectively, in 1970 and that white working men in those age ranges earn $7 and $9 per hour, respectively. If there are equal numbers of working men in each of the two age groups, then the average earnings of black men in 1970 are $6 per hour, the average earnings of white men are $8 per hour, and the 1970 black-to-white earnings ratio is .75. In 1980, working men in their thirties in 1970 will all be in their forties. Suppose that black working men so aged experience an increase in earnings from $5 to $7, while comparably aged white working men enjoy a wage increase from $7 to $10. This implies

that the earnings ratio for this continuing group of working men has fallen from $5/$7 = .71 to $7/$10 = .70. But if the entering group of black and white working men, aged 30 to 39 in 1980, have hourly earnings of $6 and $7, respectively, then the average earnings ratio has risen from .75 to $6.50/$8.50 = .76. Thus, the ratio for the group of working men present in both 1970 and 1980 has fallen, while the overall ratio has increased.

6

Do Women "Deserve"
to Earn Less than Men?

The Lord spoke to Moses and said, "When a man makes a special vow to
the Lord which requires your valuation of living persons, a male between
twenty and sixty years old shall be valued at fifty silver shekels. If it is a
female, she shall be valued at thirty shekels."
—Leviticus 27:1-4, *New English Bible*

That the value of a woman's work is about three-fifths that of a man's
seems to hold for modern as well as biblical times. Census Bureau
figures (U.S. Department of Labor, 1973) show that the ratio of average
hourly earnings of women to men was .63 in 1949, .65 in 1959, and .63
in 1969.[1] The sex-based earnings gap is larger than the earnings gap
between black and white men, and does not appear to have narrowed
much in recent decades.

In attempting to understand the lower earning status of women, some
analysts point to the fact that women are heavily concentrated into a few
job categories—secretarial work, teaching, nursing, and various service
occupations. Some of the wage gap between women and men can be
explained by these occupational differences, and it is possible to recast
the analysis of wage differentials into an examination of the process of
occupational choice. Such an analysis is rarely conclusive, however,
since job choices are influenced by prior training, socialization, future
work plans, and current job opportunities. The importance and form of

discrimination as it affects the process of job choices is virtually impossible to ascertain with available data.

An alternative view, emphasized by economists in the past decade, is the skills and attachment explanation, which gives little weight to either discrimination or the process of occupational choice, centering instead on alleged differences in the qualifications of women and men. In this view, men earn more than women because men are more attached to the labor force and acquire more job-related skills and experience and thus obtain work in the higher-paying occupations that require and use those skills. In turn, the labor market is viewed as acting "fairly" in the sense that wages are paid according to the productivity of the worker: Women are paid less because their skills and attachment to the labor force are lower, making them less productive workers.

If this is true, then the crucial question in explaining wage differentials becomes *why* women and men acquire different amounts of skills and experience. Recent versions of the skills explanation contend that skill differences are largely the result of decisions made by women who must balance the demands of market work against those of children and other work in the home. This view does not deny that occupational differences exist; rather, it interprets them as reflecting the choices of women who want jobs that accommodate their home responsibilities and do not penalize them unduly for the time they spend out of the labor force. In other words, women earn less than men because they voluntarily choose to do so.

This chapter examines the ability of the skills and attachment explanation to account for earnings differentials between women and men. The Panel Study data are uniquely suited for such an inquiry since the information they provide on the work history and labor force attachment of a large, representative sample of working women and men is much greater than that provided by any other data set.

Panel Study data show substantial differences in the average amounts of work experience that women and men have acquired and marked differences between the sexes in reported attachment to the labor force. Taken together, however, these differences account for only about one-third of the wage gap between white women and white men and only about one-quarter of the earnings differences between black women and white men. Thus, while in one sense women may "deserve" somewhat lower earnings based on their accumulated experience and job-related skills, most of the wage gap cannot be attributed to these differences.

Why Do Women Earn Less than Men?

Among the many explanations for the lower economic status of women, differences between women and men in job skills and attachment to the labor market have been given prominent attention. The skills and attachment explanation posits that most, if not all, of the earnings gap between the sexes is a consequence of the home responsibilities assumed by women. Saying that the wage differentials are deserved, however, in no way implies that the choices made by women are unwise. Quite the contrary. Women are seen as merely responding to the incentives imposed by their current responsibilities and future plans. Men faced with similar incentives would be expected to make similar choices.[2]

This version of the skills and attachment explanation has assumed a prominent place in government analysis of female/male pay differences. The *Economic Report of the President* (1974), for example, develops its explanation of pay differentials by first stating that the "traditional economic organization of the family has been marked by a specialization of function; women tend to specialize in work associated with child care and keeping up the home; men tend to specialize in labor market employment. . . . Whether it [this specialization] now reflects societal discrimination or efficiency is a matter for speculation." The *Report* next states that this sex difference in role specialization may account for much of the female/male pay differential. An analysis of the National Longitudinal Survey (NLS) by Mincer and Polachek (1974) is cited to support this point; they found that half of the wage gap between married women and married men aged 30 to 44 years could be accounted for by sex differences in the amount and value of work experience and in the penalties women incur because their skills become "rusty" when they drop out of the labor force. The *Report* suggests that much of the remaining unexplained wage differential might also be generated by sex differences in role specialization, speculating that women might "choose not to invest in training" because of the uncertainty of future work patterns. Even never-married women early in their careers "may choose not to make investments related to work because they expect to marry."

This skills explanation of the sex-based wage gap has very conservative policy implications. To the extent that female/male differentials result from voluntary choices about home and market work, programs that intervene in the hiring, promotion, and pay decisions generated by the labor market cannot be justified. Instead, policies that seek to alter the sex division of labor at home and increase the extent and continuity of women's labor force participation might be expected to reduce sex-based wage differentials more effectively.

Despite the importance given to skill and attachment explanations in governmental analyses of the female/male wage gap, there is actually no definitive evidence to support the contention that skills or attachment play a major role. Mincer and Polachek analyzed a very restricted segment of the population, married women aged 30 to 44 with children, while analyses by Sawhill (1973) and Oaxaca (1973) of less restricted populations have not confirmed the skill explanation. But these other studies have generally relied on data sources designed for other purposes, and the correspondence between available empirical measures and various theoretical concepts often becomes quite remote. For example, the empirical finding that marital status affects the relative earnings of women is often interpreted as the result of work commitment differences between married and unmarried women. But might such a marital status effect be the result of discriminatory actions on the part of the employers rather than individual or even average skill differences? It is impossible to tell.

Testing the Skills and Attachment Explanation[3]

The Panel Study data are well suited to test the skills explanation since a special questionnaire was developed in one of the years (1976) and administered not only to household heads but to wives as well. The questionnaire was designed to address many of the hypotheses regarding pay differences, and included direct questions on labor market history and interruptions, absenteeism, and self-imposed restrictions on job location and work hours. Furthermore, both women and men were asked these questions to see if the men with limitations or labor market withdrawals suffered the same wage penalties as women with corresponding behavior. Both women and men can restrict job location or work hours either because of family responsibilities or because of personal preferences. Regardless of the reason, similar restrictions should, in the absence of discrimination, bring similar wage penalties to both women and men. Also, some men may drop out of the civilian labor force for a period of years without acquiring additional job skills—perhaps for military service. All of the respondents—women and men—who dropped out of the labor force were asked whether, during the period of withdrawal, they had acquired any training or skills that would be useful on a job. If labor markets are efficient, then the wage penalty suffered by men who did not acquire useful job skills while in military service should be similar to that of women who withdrew from the labor force to raise children.

In our attempt to assess the explanatory power of the skills explanation of earnings differentials, we investigated the effects of five measures of work-related experience and attachment: education, work experience, work continuity, self-imposed work restrictions, and absenteeism.[4] If the sex based wage differential is "deserved" and if our list of experience and attachment variables is complete and well measured, then sex differentials in them should "explain" most of the gap. As was the case in the previous chapter, the contribution of a particular variable in explaining the wage gap will be the product of the actual difference in the average amount of that skill between women and men and the economic value of that skill.[5]

In discussing our results, we will first summarize the differences in average amounts of the skill measures and then present the contribution of the skill differences in explaining the wage gap. It will be shown that, while there were substantial skill differences between the sexes as predicted by the skills explanation, these differences could only account for about one-third of the total wage gap between white women and white men and only about one-fourth of the gap between black women and white men.

Education. As shown in the first three columns of the first row of Table 6.1, the average educational attainment of white women is nearly equal to that for white men, while the average attainment of black women is about one year less than that for white women. These differences between black and white women are considerably smaller than those found between black and white men in the previous chapter.

Work experience. The most obvious way in which women accommodate family responsibilities is by leaving work altogether. White and black women differed dramatically from white men in the amounts they had worked. Employed white men worked an average of 20 years, 11.3 years on jobs prior to the present one and 8.7 years, on average, in the current job. In contrast, total work experience was about 14 years for employed white women and 16 years for black women. Women had spent two to three years less time in their present employment than had white men. Furthermore, women's work experience was more likely to have involved part-time work. On the average, about 20 percent of the

Table 6.1

MEAN VALUES OF WORK SKILL MEASURES AND PERCENTAGES OF THE WAGE GAPS BETWEEN WHITE MEN AND WOMEN ACCOUNTED FOR BY EDUCATION, WORK EXPERIENCE, AND WORK CONTINUITY

Skill Measures	Average Amounts of Work Skills			Explained Percentage of the Wage Gaps Between[a]	
	White Men	White Women	Black Women	White Men and White Women	White Men and Black Women
Education (years)	12.9	12.7	11.8	2%	10%
Work Experience:					
Experience prior to present job (years)	11.3	8.1	9.3	4%	2%
Tenure in present job (years)	8.7	5.7	6.5	16%	10%
Proportion of total working years that were full time	.91	.79	.83	9%	5%
Work Continuity:					
Years out of the labor force between school and first permanent job	.7	3.2	3.1	2%	1%
Length of most recent interruption (in years)	1.0	2.5	.5	1%	0%
Two or more work interruptions	.028	.118	.037	1%	0%

Table 6.1 (Continued)

Skill Measures	Average Amounts of Work Skills			Explained Percentage of the Wage Gaps Between[a]	
	White Men	White Women	Black Women	White Men and White Women	White Men and Black Women
Self-Imposed Job Restriction:					
Placed limitations on job hours or location	.15	.34	.22	3%	0%
Working part time voluntarily	.01	.15	.09	-2%	0%
Absenteeism:					
Annual hours of absenteeism due to own illness	37	43	58	0%	0%
Annual hours of absenteeism due to illness of other family members	4	12	25	-1%	-2%
Total				35%	26%

[a]*Note:* These columns show the extent to which difference in each skill or attachment measure accounts for the total wage gap between white men and the two groups of women. The differences are valued by effects estimated from a statistical analysis that adjusts for the effects of differences in all of the other variables listed in the table.

Table reads: "Schooling of white men averaged 12.9 years, compared with averages of 12.7 and 11.8 years for white and black women, respectively. The schooling differences between white men and women accounted for 2% of the earnings gap between them. The schooling difference between white men and black women accounted for 10% of the earnings gap between those two groups."

past work experience of employed women involved part-time rather than full-time work; this compared to less than 10 percent for white men.

Work continuity. Sex differences are even more striking in the patterns of continuity of work history. More than half of all employed white men had worked continuously since leaving school.[6] White men's spells of nonwork since leaving school were quite short; they were concentrated at the start of their work careers, usually beginning before age 25, and very often involved the acquisition of job-related skills. Less than 3 percent of white men reported interrupting their careers more than once, compared with 12 percent of white women. But only 36 percent of employed white women had worked continuously since completing school. White women's labor force withdrawals tended to be long, to occur at all points in the work cycle, and typically did not involve the acquisition of job-related skills. Black women's work history patterns fell somewhere in between those of white women and white men. More black women (42 percent) than white women (36 percent) had worked continuously since school completion; black women were more likely to have withdrawn from work early in their careers, and black women's labor force withdrawals were shorter.

Self-imposed restrictions on labor supply.[7] A second way in which women accommodate family responsibilities is by restricting where, when, and how much they will work. One in three white women and one in five black women reported that self-imposed limitations on job hours or location were factors in taking their present job; only one in seven white men reported imposing such limitations. Women were also more likely to report that they were working less than full time out of personal choice. Compared to only 1 percent of white men, about 15 percent of white women and 9 percent of black women voluntarily worked less than 30 hours per week in 1975.[8]

Absenteeism. Finally, women might accommodate family responsibilities at the expense of work duties. For instance, women might be less reliable or dependable employees than men. This possibility is reflected in worker absenteeism—particularly in absenteeism due to the illness of other family members. About 20 to 25 percent of all employed women reported missing some work in 1975 because of another family member's illness. And women who missed work to care for other family members missed a fair amount of work; an average of 57 hours a year for white women and 103 hours a year for black women.[9] Moreover, about 65 percent of all women who missed work to care for family members did so to care for sick children. Few white men (about 10 percent) ever missed work to care for other family members; those white men who did miss work for this reason typically did so to care for their wives.

Sex differences in absenteeism due to the individual's own illness were much smaller. The average white man missed 37 hours in 1975, the average white woman missed 43 hours, and the average black woman missed 55 hours.

Accounting for the Sex-Based Wage Gap

Although white men differed considerably from white and black women in a number of ways related to skills and attachment, this does not necessarily "explain" all of the earnings advantages that white men enjoyed. Women's lesser work experience and work continuity, their greater self-imposed labor supply restrictions, and their higher absenteeism rates would explain the gap only if these characteristics in themselves had substantial effects on earnings. If, for example, among all workers, those who placed restrictions on their work hours or job location were *not* paid less than other workers, then the fact that women, on average, tended to self-impose more restrictions would not explain why they earned less than white men.

The last two columns of Table 6.1 show the results of combining information on differences in the amounts of education, work experience, work continuity, job restrictions, and absenteeism across the two sex subgroups with the estimated effects of these factors on earnings.[10] The figures in those columns are estimates of the fraction of the wage gaps between white men and the two groups of women that is explained by each of the skill measures.

Even though additional years of education increased earnings, the average educational attainment of white women and white men was so similar that their schooling differences accounted for only 2 percent of the sex-based wage gap between them, while the one-year difference in schooling between white men and black women explained 10 percent of their wage gap.

As expected, differences in amount of work experience accounted for a significant portion of the wage gaps between white women and white men, largely because women acquired less tenure and were more likely to have worked part time. Altogether, differences in amounts of work experience accounted for 29 percent of the wage gap between white women and white men, and 17 percent of the gap between black women and white men.

Unexpectedly, the large differences that existed in work continuity did little to explain the wage gap between white men and white and black women. Although discontinuity did lower the amount of women's work experience, the extra penalty because skills became rusty was very small. We examined the effects of three kinds of labor force withdrawals: those that followed school completion (years between school and work), interruptions that occurred after a work career had begun (length of most recent interruption), and multiple interruptions (two or more). After adjusting the effects of lost experience, labor force withdrawals did not consistently lower wages for either white men or for white or black women; indeed, white men's wages were never affected, and black women's wages were rarely affected by labor force withdrawals. For white women who dropped out of the labor force between school completion and the start of their first job, expected wages dropped slightly for each year they did not work (about eight-tenths of a percent per year); but white women who began work after completing school and who later interrupted their work careers suffered no long-term penalties.

A more complete look at the wage changes associated with labor market interruptions and part- and full-time work is presented in Corcoran, Duncan, and Ponza (1983). Building on the work of Mincer and Ofek (1982), they analyze patterns of wages and work hours over the thirteen-year period from 1967 to 1979. Like Mincer and Ofek, they find that the hourly earnings of women who are reentering the labor force after taking some time out are indeed lower than when they left. But this wage gap narrows rapidly because the wage growth of the reentering workers is so great, especially if they work full time. Mincer and Ofek argue that the rapid wage increases come about because the women who drop out can easily restore the skills they have lost once they reenter the labor market. The rapid wage growth may also be due to the sorting process by which both employers and employees try to find the best match between worker and job. For example, many jobs have probationary periods with low pay that become regular jobs with higher pay once the probationary period is over. In any case, the long-run effect on wages of taking time out of the labor market is small, and does not account for much of the wage gap between women and men.

Another surprising result is that the differences in self-imposed job restrictions and absenteeism to care for other family members explained almost none of the wage gap. Women and white men who were frequently absent from work or who had imposed limitations on work hours or job locations did not earn consistently less than did equally qualified workers who imposed no limitations and had attended work regularly.[11] Even women who were voluntarily working part time earned no less per hour than other women.

Apparently women do indeed earn less than men because they have acquired less work experience and have assumed more home responsibilities. But, taken together, these differences account for only about one-third of the wage gap between white women and white men, and only about one-quarter of the wage gap between black women and white men.[12] Before dismissing the skills explanation as relatively unimportant, however, we should consider whether our skill variables are sufficiently comprehensive and precisely measured to do justice to this theory.

One troubling issue is the prominent omission from our analysis of the possible consequences of family migration, given the argument that for married couples such moves are more likely to be determined by the career interests of the husband than by those of the wife.[13] If these moves cause women to leave their jobs, the effects should show up in our measures of time spent in and out of the labor force. For couples who moved, if the wife resumed work one might expect that her wages would fall relative to those of her husband. But when Hill (1978, pp. 173–6) compared the changes in relative earnings of couples who had migrated to those that had not, she failed to find significant differences.

It is also possible that the *prospect* of migration may cause women to choose lower-paying, less specialized occupations that will be in demand anywhere. This possible cause of lower earnings for women was not included among our skill and attachment measures. Measuring its effects is difficult and requires a general theory of occupational selection based on prospective migration and other economic incentives, on socialization, and on possible involuntary, institutional factors as well. The fact that women are overrepresented in many jobs with unspecialized skills can be explained in many ways other than voluntary, skill-based ones.

A second issue, measurement error, is also troubling. It is easy to point out instances where the correspondence between concept and measure is indirect; an obvious example is the use of years of work experience as a measure of the amount of work skills acquired in past and present jobs. Although it is never possible to rule out the possible effects of measurement error, there is a point at which such effects can be judged too unlikely to affect the basic results. By designing our questionnaire to test the skills and attachment explanation of female/ male wage differentials, we were able to measure the components of work history with much greater precision than in the past, and to measure more of them as well. Our expanded list accounted for little more of the wage gap than have smaller lists with less precise measurement. At some point, the researcher must conclude that a line of inquiry is not sufficiently powerful to account for all of the observed earnings differentials. We believe that the skills explanation has reached such a point. While skill differences between women and men do indeed exist and do account for some of the wage gap, the chances that they account for most of it appear quite remote.

Alternative Explanations

Once we accept the conclusion that skills differences don't explain all of the gap, then alternative explanations must be considered. There are two major kinds of explanations—discrimination and socialization. Discrimination may take many forms, each with different implications for policies that might be designed to combat it. For instance, suppose women earn less than men because employers pay men more than equally qualified women who are working at the same job. In this case, enforcing laws requiring equal pay for equal work would be the primary strategy to equalize the wages of women and men. But suppose employers deny women access to well-paid jobs with advancement opportunities. Policies of equal pay for equal work would be ineffective in this case; instead, the focus of policy efforts would need to be on equalizing opportunities in hiring and promotions. Exactly how one would design these policies depends upon the nature of discrimination.

It is also possible that earnings differences might persist even if skill differences and discrimination were eliminated. Socialization may lead women to aspire to lower-paying jobs quite independently of the skills they acquire or the actual discrimination they may face. Here the policy prescriptions are even more difficult and require an understanding of how and when career aspirations are formed and whether they are subject to change.

But it is also quite possible that the conventional wisdom about the importance of "female" versus "male" jobs has been overstated. In the first place, there is only weak evidence that among equally qualified and experienced women, those who work in a typically female occupation earn less. Secondly, longitudinal data (Corcoran et al., 1983) suggest that there is substantial movement of women between typically female and male jobs, indicating that many women are not locked unalterably into the female-dominated jobs.[14] But perhaps most important is evidence that knowledge of how much time a woman works is much more important in understanding her pattern of wage change than is knowledge of what kind of job she held. Indeed, Corcoran et al. found that part-time work did not lead to significant wage growth in *either* typically female or typically male jobs while years of full-time work had similar beneficial wage effects within both job types.

Taken together, these findings suggest that we should move beyond the broad stereotypes and examine specific aspects of the job market dynamics for women and men, such as patterns of job access and the characteristics of the jobs held by women and men. Additional Panel Study analysis has focused on three such aspects—the information and influence networks that might have been used in obtaining the jobs, the authority over others conferred by the job, and the training content of the job. None of these presents a complete picture, merely pieces of the puzzle.

"Old Boy" Networks

Past research has shown that many, if not most, workers hear about jobs informally. Some additional research has shown that jobs obtained informally generally pay higher wages than jobs obtained through formal channels.[15] Most of this research was restricted to male workers, however. In the eleventh (1978) interviewing wave of the Panel Study, we asked all working women and men under age 45 who headed households how they (and all working wives) heard about and obtained their first jobs with their current employers. There were small but consistent differences in the use of informal information and influence channels between white men and each of the two groups of white and black women. Whereas 52 percent of the white men heard about their jobs from friends or relatives, the comparable fractions for white and black women were 47 and 43 percent, respectively. Larger differences show up in the responses to questions about whether they received help in getting the jobs. Two-fifths of the white men responded affirmatively, compared to one-third of the two groups of women. Nearly one-fifth of the white men both knew someone who worked at their future place of employment and were helped in getting the job by someone with "much say." This fraction was 50 percent higher than that of white women and nearly three times higher than for black women. Surprisingly, workers in all three groups who used informal information or influence channels did not appear to have higher-paying jobs than those who used formal channels. Thus, the relatively small differences in access coupled with the lack of wage effects suggest that differential access to informal channels of information and influence is not a primary cause of lower earnings for women.

Authority

Among the many job characteristics that seem to give rise to wage differentials, one of the most important appears to be authority over the work of others. Using information from the 1977 interviewing wave of the Panel Study, Hill and Morgan (1979) found that the earnings of those who merely supervised the work of others differed little from comparable workers without supervisory responsibilities. However, having some say over the pay or promotion of others was associated with a 20 percent higher pay rate.

There are several explanations for the importance of supervisory authority. An economist schooled in conventional theory might argue that authority is granted to those with greater knowledge of the needs of the firm and the abilities of fellow workers, so that authority can be seen as a way in which the firm puts that knowledge to work, and the wage premium is thus a kind of reward for those skills. Or it might be argued that positions of authority may be open to all but that the responsibilities they impose are so undesirable that a wage premium is required to induce workers to take them.

Alternative theories assign a much more central role to authority structures, seeing them as the means of maintaining an existing social or economic order, often implying the existence of some form of discrimination or inequity. For example, from a sociologist's perspective, a rigid, hierarchical authority structure operates to legitimize the lower status and economic position of many workers. To a Marxist, the authority structure ensures that the existing class structure is preserved from one generation to the next. Feminist theory would add that, in a patriarchal society, authority structures perpetuate men's control over economic resources so that women are kept economically dependent on men and will accept subordinate and supportive roles relative to men of any class or status. All such theories would predict that access to authority roles would tend to be limited to those seen as likely to carry out the function of maintaining a status quo.

Regardless of the cause, there are striking differences between the fractions of women and men who supervise other workers and those who make decisions regarding their pay and promotions. While nearly half of all male workers reported supervising at least one other worker, the comparable fraction for women was barely one-quarter.[16] For those having say over pay or promotions, the respective fractions were about one-quarter for men and one-tenth for women.

Several factors were found to increase one's chances of being in a position of having say over pay or promotions. Additional years of tenure on the current job increased these chances much more than did general years of labor market experience. Educational level was also instrumental, but much more so for men than women. Additional years of both education and tenure increased the chance of a man being authorized to make decisions about pay or promotions by three percent—roughly three times greater than the effect for women. In other words, it appears that education and tenure do not lead to authority for women in the same way they do for men.

Access to Jobs with Training

A dominant theme of the skills explanation is that training and other skill differences between the sexes are largely the result of voluntary choice rather than institutional forces and labor market discrimination. Direct questions about the training content of jobs were included in the 1976 questionnaire, and the incidence of training was related to a set of variables reflecting voluntary and involuntary factors that may affect the training decision.[17] The results did provide some evidence of the skills explanation's assumption that training is considered as an investment. The potential length of time over which a training investment might yield returns was an important factor in explaining whether an individual was found to be in the training phase of his or her job. For white women, the expectation of having more children was a deterrent to training. On the other hand, it was found that training may also be affected by institutional forces. The length of time spent in the labor force and with the current employer generally led to training in a much more direct way for white men than for women, even after differences in labor market commitment were taken into account. Thus, women were not advanced to new positions with longer training periods as rapidly as were men.

Summary and Implications

Do women workers "deserve" to fare badly relative to men? Our findings suggest that much of the sex-based wage gap is indeed not deserved. Although women do earn less than men because of the home-related responsibilities they assume, taken together, these responsibilities account for only about one-third of the wage gap between women and men. Although the skill and attachment differences that arise from the fact that women in our society generally do spend a considerable amount of time out of the labor force may not have been measured precisely or, in a few cases, may have been omitted altogether, it seems unlikely that anyone will be able to find that they account for most of the wage gap. Indeed, one might well argue that our one-third figure is too large since sex differences in several of our qualifications measures might themselves be the direct result of discrimination or the results of rational responses to perceived market discrimination.

Although much of the wage gap was unexplained by sex differences in skills, our results do suggest that there may be ways in which working couples could combine their family and work roles more efficiently and thus reduce at least some of the "deserved" portion of the earnings gap. We found that women earned less because they typically had less work experience and were more likely to have worked part time than white men. Policies to reduce these differences in work patterns might include paid parental leaves for either parent rather than just the mother, more flexibility in work hours, increasing the availability of part-time work in the more prestigious occupations, or shared jobs. The flexible timing policies would seem especially useful since most of the women (and men) who restrict their job search do so because of concern for the timing of hours rather than the volume of hours or job location.

But policies aimed at reducing the deserved portion of the earnings gap will, at best, only close part of the total gap. We found that even after adjusting for sex differences on an extensive list of qualifications, white men earned substantially more than did women. Those who claim that the labor market treats workers fairly in the sense that equally qualified workers are paid equally are likely to be wrong. Our results also suggest that policies aimed at equalizing skills as the major way of reducing economic inequality between women and men workers are misdirected. Policies that promote the educational attainment and training of women or that seek to alter the sex division of labor within the home will not eliminate most of the wage gap between men and women.

If skills do not "explain" most of the wage gap, then what does explain it? It is difficult to test for the importance of the two major competing explanations—discrimination and socialization. White men's current jobs provided at least twice as much authority and on-the-job training as did women's, and both training and authority increased wages. Our evidence indicates that women did not receive the same opportunities for training and supervision as equally qualified men. Does this occur because women deliberately avoid these jobs, or because they are systematically excluded from them? In order to reach a definite conclusion, we need information on the behavior of firms and on the aspirations and early labor market behavior of men and women. We suspect that there is some truth to both the discrimination and the socialization explanations. The role of discrimination has been substantiated in a number of cases in courts and before the Equal Employment Opportunity Commission, in which women have proven the existence of past discrimination and employers have been ordered to pay substantial sums and even to restructure employment practices and policies. The role of socialization is confirmed by psychologists and sociologists who have demonstrated that boys and girls develop very different career aspirations and that these differences widen with age.

If firms do treat equally qualified women and men differently in their hiring, pay, and promotion decisions, then policies that will intervene in these decisions need to be considered. There are at least two different approaches to this. First, one might try to open up traditionally "male" jobs to women. Second, one might try to insure that "female" jobs pay as much as "male" jobs whenever the relative amount and quality of work performed is equal. Both of these strategies have problems.

Affirmative action programs and the guidelines established by the Equal Employment Opportunities Commission are aimed at opening the "good" jobs to women. But policies of this sort are bound to be costly and controversial even in the best of times and even more so during slack economic conditions. Unemployed or unpromoted men do not look with favor upon women taking "their" jobs. Indeed, this competition for jobs might well cause a backlash of old stereotypes about women belonging in the home—thus reinforcing conventional sex-role socialization. A trend in this direction is already apparent in recent policy statements by various conservative groups and in such influential books as *Wealth and Poverty* (Gilder, 1981).

Designing and implementing policies aimed at ensuring equal pay for comparable work will also raise problems.[18] Perhaps the most serious problem is developing a method for rating jobs so that comparisons can be made in the first place. Once one decides what job characteristics to include in these comparisons, there is still the problem of rating these characteristics. The typical technique used in many job evaluation systems is to pick a set of benchmark jobs and use market wages to set weights. If these wage rates include bias from discrimination, this bias will be incorporated in the weights. Even if one could devise a reasonable job evaluation procedure, there remains the problem of applying it to all jobs in the country. This would likely involve exceedingly large administrative costs.

Policies that attempt to intervene in the socialization process will be even more controversial than policies that intervene in the labor market. Government interference with the ways in which parents raise their children is neither likely nor desirable. On the other hand, reducing sex stereotyping in schoolbooks or developing school guidance programs that emphasize nontraditional jobs for women and men may be more acceptable. And it may be that policies aimed at increasing the variety of work available to women through shared jobs, flexible hours, or promoting equal opportunities will in turn affect sex-role socialization. If girls and boys see women and men in a variety of roles, this may widen children's perspectives about their future roles as adults.

Policies that attack discrimination directly or that influence the pattern of socialization will be more controversial than training and education policies. But the long-run costs of ignoring the pay gap between women and men may be even greater. Women are currently underemployed relative to their qualifications. Keeping them in jobs where they cannot utilize their skills and abilities reduces their productivity and must result in substantial economic costs to society due to inefficient utilization of its labor resources. Furthermore, a continuing failure to reach society's widely endorsed goal of equal opportunity in the case of women imposes very different and possibly much more serious costs to society—costs that arise when a persistently mistreated group begins to question the legitimacy of the economic system that sets the labor market rules.

Notes

[1]These ratios have been adjusted for differences in educational attainment. Fuchs (1974) finds that adjustments for schooling and age produce hourly wage ratios of .61 in 1959 and .64 in 1969, and cites the biblical reference that opens this chapter.

[2]It is possible that the reduced incentive for women to acquire skills is reinforced by the fact that discrimination reduces the likely reward to those skills. This element is not an integral part of the skills explanation although it is believed by some of its proponents.

[3]This section summarizes material presented in Duncan and Corcoran (1979) and Corcoran (1979).

[4]Omitted from this list are concrete kinds of skills such as typing speed and managerial acumen. To include them would introduce the problems associated with occupational choice. If a woman with a given typing speed earned the same as a man with equal speed but much less than the average man with equal education, years in the labor force, and labor market attachment, should this be taken as evidence that the labor market is "fair" or "unfair"? The view taken in this chapter and, indeed, in the skills explanation, is that women and men who are identical in their educational levels, their experience, and their past, present, and future attachment to the labor force ought to be earning similar rates of pay

[5]Suppose that the average education level of men exceeded that of women by one year. The contribution of that difference in explaining the wage gap will depend upon the value of a year's worth of education. If the average wages of women and men differ by $2.00 per hour and an additional year of education is "worth" $2.00 per hour, then all of the wage gap can be explained by the education difference. But if an additional year of education is worth only $.25 per hour, then only one-eighth of the gap would be accounted for by the education difference.

[6]Some of the information cited here does not appear explicitly on Table 6.1, but is detailed in Corcoran (1978).

[7]The label "self-imposed restrictions" should not be construed to imply that such choices are all freely made, independent of other constraints. The very concept of "women's family responsibilities" implies conditions that may restrict women's freedom to work in the labor market—for example, the unavailability of adequate, affordable child-care; or perhaps expectations or demands imposed by a husband or other family members.

[8]Specifically, the situation was considered voluntary if individuals reported either that more work was available on their job so that they could have worked more if they had wanted to or if they reported that they would not have liked more work if they could have found it.

[9]The figures on absenteeism shown in Table 6.1 are lower than those given in text since the former are averages for *all* women in the group, not just for those who missed some work.

[10]Effects are estimated from a statistical analysis that adjusts for differences in all other variables listed in Table 6.1. Specifically, ordinary least-squares regressions were run separately for the three groups of workers on a linear and additive model with the natural logarithm of the 1975 hourly wage rate as dependent variables and the independent variables listed in Table 6.1.

[11]Since it takes time for employers to adjust pay and promotion decisions in response to individual performance, the result that current pay and absenteeism are unrelated may not be surprising. However, additional analysis has also shown that wages are not related to *past* absenteeism.

[12]The extent to which differences in skills account for earnings differences depends somewhat on the exact way in which skill factors are measured and included in the analysis. Corcoran and Duncan (1979) found that skill factors accounted for 44 percent of the wage gap between white women and white men and 32 percent of the gap between black women and white men. In no case did skill factors account for more than 50 percent of the wage gap.

[13]Mincer (1978) attaches considerable importance to this possibility, arguing that "migration ranks next to child rearing as an important dampening influence in the life cycle wage evolution of women" (p.771).

[14]Corcoran et al. looked at white and black women who had worked at least 250 hours during calendar years 1975 and 1979. Of those white women who were found to be working in female-dominated job categories 1975, 31 percent were found to be working in male-dominated job categories four years later in 1979. For black women, the comparable figure is 25 percent.

[15]Corcoran, Datcher, and Duncan (1980) review these studies and detail the analysis presented in this paragraph.

[16]These are household heads and wives between the ages of 18 and 64 who were not self-employed.

[17]This analysis is presented in Duncan and Hoffman (1979).

[18]The discussion in this paragraph is largely based on a discussion with Dr. Heidi Hartmann of the National Academy of Science.

References

Anderson, Martin. 1978. *Welfare*. Stanford, CA: Hoover Institution Press.

Anderson-Khleif, Susan. 1976. "Income Packaging and Life-Style in Welfare Families and in Female-headed Families: Major Themes." Mimeographed. Cambridge, MA: Joint Center for Urban Studies.

Andrisani, Paul J. 1976. "Discrimination, Segmentation, and Upward Mobility; A Longitudinal Approach to the Dual Labor Market Theory." Mimeographed. Philadelphia: Temple University.

———. 1977. "Internal–External Attitudes, Personal Initiative, and the Labor Market Experience of Black and White Men." *Journal of Human Resources* 12:308-328.

———. 1981. "Internal–External Attitudes, Sense of Efficacy, and Labor Market Experience: A Reply to Duncan and Morgan." *Journal of Human Resources* 16:658–666.

Auletta, Ken. 1982. *The Underclass*, New York: Random House.

Baerwaldt, Nancy A., and James N. Morgan. 1973. "Trends in Interfamily Transfers." In *Surveys of Consumers 1971–1972*, edited by Lewis Mandell et al., pp. 205–232. Ann Arbor: Institute for Social Research, The University of Michigan.

Bane, Mary Jo. 1976. *Here to Stay: American Families in the Twentieth Century*. New York: Basic Books.

Bane, Mary Jo, and David Ellwood. 1982. "Slipping Into and Out of Poverty: The Dynamics of Spells." Mimeographed. Cambridge, MA: Harvard University.

Becker, Gary S. 1957. *Economics of Discrimination*. Chicago: University of Chicago Press.

———. 1975. *Human Capital*. 2nd ed. New York: Columbia University Press.

Boskin, M., and F. Nold. 1975. "A Markov Model of Turnover in Aid to Families with Dependent Children." *Journal of Human Resources* 10:507–518.

Bowles, Samuel, and Herbert Gintis. 1972–73. "IQ in the U.S. Class Structure." Parts 1, 2. *Social Policy* 4, 5:65–96.

Browning, Edgar K. 1975. *Redistribution and the Welfare System*. Washington, D.C.: American Enterprise Institute.

Butler, Richard J. 1982. "Estimating Wage Discrimination in the Labor Market." *Journal of Human Resources* 17:606–621.

Coe, Richard D. 1978. "Dependency and Poverty in the Short and Long Run." In *Five Thousand American Families—Patterns of Economic Progress*, Vol. 6, edited by Greg J. Duncan and James N. Morgan. Ann Arbor: Institute for Social Research, The University of Michigan.

———. 1979. "Participation in the Food Stamp Program Among the Poverty Population." In *Five Thousand American Families—Patterns of Economic Progress*, Vol. 7, edited by Greg J. Duncan and James N. Morgan. Ann Arbor: Institute for Social Research, The University of Michigan.

———. 1981. "A Preliminary Empirical Examination of the Dynamics of Welfare Use." In *Five Thousand American Families—Patterns of Economic Progress*, Vol. 9, edited by Martha S. Hill and James N. Morgan. Ann Arbor: Institute for Social Research, The University of Michigan.

Corcoran, Mary. 1978. "Work Experience, Work Interruption, and Wages." In *Five Thousand American Families—Patterns of Economic Progress*, Vol. 6, edited by Greg J. Duncan and James N. Morgan, pp. 47–104. Ann Arbor: Institute for Social Research, The University of Michigan.

———. 1979 "Work Experience, Labor Force Withdrawals, and Women's Wages: Empirical Results Using the 1976 Panel of Income Dynamics." In *Women in the Labor Market*, edited by Cynthia B. Lloyd, Emily S. Andrews, and Curtis L. Gilroy. New York: Columbia University Press.

Corcoran, Mary, and Linda P. Datcher. 1981. "Intergenerational Status Transmission and the Process of Individual Attainment." In *Five Thousand American Families—Patterns of Economic Progress*, Vol. 9, edited by Martha S. Hill, Daniel H. Hill, and James N. Morgan, pp. 169–206. Ann Arbor: Institute for Social Research, The University of Michigan.

Corcoran, Mary, Linda Datcher, and Greg J. Duncan. 1980. "Information and Influence Networks in the Labor Market." In *Five Thousand American Families—Patterns of Economic Progress*, Vol. 8, edited by Greg J. Duncan and James N. Morgan, pp. 1–38. Ann Arbor: Institute for Social Research, The University of Michigan.

Corcoran, Mary, and Greg J. Duncan. 1979. "Work History, Labor Force Attachment, and Earnings Differences Between the Races and Sexes." *Journal of Human Resources* 14:3–20.

Corcoran, Mary, Greg J. Duncan, and Michael Ponza. 1983. "Work Experience, Job Segregation, and Wages." In *Five Thousand American Families— Patterns of Economic Progress*, Vol. 10, edited by Greg J. Duncan and James N. Morgan. Ann Arbor: Institute for Social Research, The University of Michigan.

Corcoran, Mary, and Martha S. Hill. 1979. "The Incidence and Consequences of Short- and Long-Run Unemployment." In *Five Thousand American Fami-*

lies— *Patterns of Economic Progress*, Vol. 7, edited by Greg J. Duncan and James N. Morgan, pp. 1–62. Ann Arbor: Institute for Social Research, The University of Michigan.

———. 1980. "Unemployment and Poverty." *Social Service Review* 54:407–413.

Datcher, Linda. 1981. "Racial Differences in the Effects of Background on Achievement." Mimeographed. Ann Arbor: Institute for Social Research, The University of Michigan.

———. 1982. "Effects of Community and Family Background on Achievement." *Review of Economics and Statistics* 64:32–41.

———. 1983. "Racial Differences in the Persistence of Affluence." In *Five Thousand American Families—Patterns of Economic Progress*, Vol. 10, edited by Greg J. Duncan and James N. Morgan. Ann Arbor: Institute for Social Research, The University of Michigan.

Dickinson, Jonathan. 1974. "Labor Supply of Family Members." In *Five Thousand American Families—Patterns of Economic Progress*, Vol. 1, edited by James N. Morgan, et al., pp. 177–250. Ann Arbor: Institute for Social Research, The University of Michigan.

Doeringer, Peter B., and Michael J. Piore. 1971. *Internal Labor Markets and Manpower Analysis*. Lexington, MA: Heath-Lexington Books.

Duncan, Greg J. 1977. "Paths to Economic Well-Being." In *Five Thousand American Families—Patterns of Economic Progress*, Vol. 5, edited by Greg J. Duncan and James N. Morgan, pp. 167–222. Ann Arbor: Institute for Social Research, The University of Michigan.

Duncan, Greg J., and Saul D. Hoffman. 1978. "Training and Earnings." In *Five Thousand American Families—Patterns of Economic Progress*, Vol. 6, edited by Greg J. Duncan and James N. Morgan, pp. 105–150. Ann Arbor: Institute for Social Research, The University of Michigan.

———. 1979. "On-the-Job Training and Earnings Differences by Race and Sex." *Review of Economics and Statistics* 61:594–603.

———. 1981a. "The Incidence and Wage Effects of Overeducation." *Economics of Education Review* 1:75-86.

———. 1981b. "Dynamics of Wage Change." In *Five Thousand American Families—Patterns of Economic Progress*, Vol. 9, edited by Martha S. Hill, Daniel H. Hill, and James N. Morgan. Ann Arbor: Institute for Social Research, The University of Michigan.

———. 1983. "A New Look at the Causes of the Improved Economic Status of Black Workers." *Journal of Human Resources* 18(2).

Duncan, Greg J., and Jeffrey K. Liker. 1983. "Disentangling the Efficacy–Earnings Relationship." In *Five Thousand American Families—Patterns of Economic Progress*, Vol. 10, edited by Greg J. Duncan and James N. Morgan. Ann Arbor: Institute for Social Research, The University of Michigan.

Duncan, Greg J., and James N. Morgan. 1980. "The Incidence and Some Consequences of Major Life Events." In *Five Thousand American Families—Patterns of Economic Progress*, Vol. 8, edited by Greg J. Duncan and James N. Morgan, pp. 183–241. Ann Arbor: Institute for Social Research, The University of Michigan.

————. 1981*a*. "Persistence and Change In Economic Status and the Role of Changing Family Composition." In *Five Thousand American Families— Patterns of Economic Progress*, Vol. 9, edited by Martha S. Hill, Daniel H. Hill, and James N. Morgan. Ann Arbor: Institute for Social Research, The University of Michigan.

————. 1981*b*. "Sense of Efficacy and Subsequent Change in Earnings: A Replication." *Journal of Human Resources* 16:649–657.

————,eds. 1977. *Five Thousand American Families—Patterns of Economic Progress*, Vol. 5. Ann Arbor: Institute for Social Research, The University of Michigan.

————,eds. 1978. *Five Thousand American Families—Patterns of Economic Progress*, Vol. 6, Chapters I–V. Ann Arbor: Institute for Social Research, The University of Michigan.

Duncan, O.D. 1969. "Inheritance of Poverty or Inheritance of Race?" In *On Understanding Poverty*, edited by David P. Moynihan. New York: Basic Books.

Economic Report of the President. 1974. Washington, D.C.: U.S. Government Printing Office.

Espenshade, Thomas J. 1979. "The Economic Consequences of Divorce." *Journal of Marriage and the Family* 41:615–625.

Featherman, David L., and Robert M. Hauser. 1976. "Changes in the Socioeconomic Stratification of the Races, 1962–1973." *American Journal of Sociology* 82:621–51.

Freeman, Richard B. 1973. "The Changing Labor Market for Black Americans." *Brookings Papers on Economic Activity* 1973(1):67–120. Washington, D.C.: Brookings Institution.

————. 1978. "Black Economic Progress After 1964: Who Has Gained and Why?" Paper presented at National Bureau of Economic Research Conference on Low-Income Labor Markets, University of Chicago.

Fuchs, Victor R. 1971. "Differences in Hourly Earnings Between Men and Women." *Monthly Labor Review* 94(5):9–15.

————. 1974. "Recent Trends and Long-Run Prospects for Female Earnings." *American Economic Review* 64:236–242.

Gilder, George. 1981. *Wealth and Poverty*. New York: Basic Books.

Goldberger, Arthur S. 1977. "Twins Methods: A Skeptical View." In *Kinometrics: The Determinants of Socioeconomic Success Within and Between Families*, edited by Paul Taubman. New York: North-Holland.

Gronau, Reuben. 1980. "Home Production—A Forgotten Industry." *Review of Economics and Statistics* 62:408–416.

Hall, Robert E. 1973. "Wages, Income, and Hours of Work in the U.S. Labor Force." In *Income Maintenance and Labor Supply*, edited by Glen Cain and Harold Watts, p. 393. Chicago: Rand-McNally.

Harrison, Bennett. 1977. "Labor Market Structure and the Relationship Between Work and Welfare." Mimeographed. Cambridge: Department of Urban Studies and Planning, Massachusetts Institute of Technology.

Hausman, Jerry A. 1981. "Labor Supply." In *How Taxes Affect Economic Behavior*, edited by Henry J. Aaron and Joseph A. Pechman, pp. 27–72. Washington, D.C.: Brookings Institution.

Haworth, Joan, James Gwartney, and Charles Haworth. "Earnings, Productivity, and Changes in Employment Discrimination During the 1960's." *American Economic Review* 65:158–168.

Heckman, James J. 1978. "Longitudinal Studies in Labor Economics: A Methodological Review." Mimeographed. Chicago: University of Chicago.

Heckman, James J., and Thomas E. MacCurdy. 1981. "New Methods for Estimating Labor Supply Functions: A Survey." In *Research in Labor Economics*, Vol. 4, edited by R.G. Ehrenberg. Greenwich, CT: JAI Press.

Heckman, James J., and Robert J. Willis. 1977. "A Beta-Logistic Model for the Analysis of Sequential Labor Force Participation by Married Women." *Journal of Political Economy* 85:27–58.

Hill, Martha S. 1978. "Self-Imposed Limitations on Work Schedule and Job Location." In *Five Thousand American Families—Patterns of Economic Progress*, Vol. 6, edited by Greg J. Duncan and James N. Morgan, pp. 151–194. Ann Arbor: Institute for Social Research, The University of Michigan.

———. 1981. "Some Dynamic Aspects of Poverty." In *Five Thousand American Families—Patterns of Economic Progress*, Vol. 9, edited by Martha S. Hill, Daniel H. Hill, and James N. Morgan. Ann Arbor: Institute for Social Research, The University of Michigan.

Hill, Martha S., and Mary Corcoran. 1979. "Unemployment Among Family Men: A Ten-Year Longitudinal Study." *Monthly Labor Review* 102(11):19–23.

Hill, Martha S., and James N. Morgan. 1979. "Dimensions of Occupation." In *Five Thousand American Families—Patterns of Economic Progress*, Vol. 7, edited by Greg J. Duncan and James N. Morgan, pp. 293–334. Ann Arbor: Institute for Social Research, The University of Michigan.

Hoffman, Saul D. 1977a. "Marital Instability and the Economic Status of Women." *Demography* 14.67–70.

———. 1977b. "Patterns of Change in Individual Earnings." In *Five Thousand American Families—Patterns of Economic Progress*, Vol. 5, edited by Greg J. Duncan and James N. Morgan, pp. 223–248. Ann Arbor: Institute for Social Research, The University of Michigan.

———. 1979. "Black–White Life-Cycle Earnings Differences and the Vintage Hypothesis: A Longitudinal Analysis." *American Economic Review* 69:855–867.

Hoffman, Saul D., and John W. Holmes. 1976. "Husbands, Wives, and Divorce." In *Five Thousand American Families—Patterns of Economic Progress*, Vol. 4, edited by Greg J. Duncan and James N. Morgan. Ann Arbor: Institute for Social Research, The University of Michigan.

Hutchens, Robert M. 1981. "Entry and Exit Transitions in a Government Transfer Program: The Case of Aid to Families with Dependent Children." *Journal of Human Resources* 16:217–237.

Juster, F. Thomas, 1979. "The Psychology of Inflation: I. Why is Inflation Bad?" *Economic Outlook USA* 6:16–17.

———,ed. 1975. *Education, Income, and Human Behavior*. New York: McGraw-Hill.

Kerr, Clark. 1954. "The Balkanization of Labor Markets." In *Labor Mobility and*

Economic Opportunity, edited by E. Wight Bakke. Cambridge, MA: MIT Press.

Lane, Jonathan P. 1981. "The Findings of the Panel Study of Income Dynamics about the AFDC Program. Mimeographed. Washington, D.C.: Assistant Secretary for Planning and Evaluation, Department of Health and Human Services.

Lane, Jonathan P., and James N. Morgan. 1975. "Patterns of Change in Economic Status and Family Structure." In *Five Thousand American Families— Patterns of Economic Progress*, Vol. 3, edited by Greg J. Duncan and James N. Morgan. Ann Arbor: Institute for Social Research, The University of Michigan.

Lazear, Edward. 1979. "The Narrowing of the Black-White Differentials Is Illusory." *American Economic Review* 69:555–564.

Levy, Frank. 1976. "How Big is the American Underclass?" Rev. version. Mimeographed. Washington, D.C.: The Urban Institute.

———. 1980. "The Intergenerational Transfer of Poverty." Working Paper 1241–02. Mimeographed. Washington, D.C.: The Urban Institute.

Lewis, Oscar. 1968. *La Vida*. London: Panther Books.

Lillard, Lee A., and Robert J. Willis. 1978. "Dynamic Aspects of Earnings Mobility." *Econometrica* 46:1013–29.

Loury, Glenn C. 1976. "Essays in the Theory of the Distribution of Income." Unpublished Ph.D. dissertation. Cambridge: Massachusetts Institute of Technology.

———. 1981. "Race and Economic Policy: Responsibilities of the Individual and the State." Presented at Sloan Foundation Lecture Series on Business and Economics, Morehouse College, Atlanta, Georgia, March 24, 1981.

Loury, Glenn C., and Jerome M. Culp. 1979. "Impact of Affirmative Action on Equal Opportunity: A New Look." Mimeographed. Ann Arbor: Economics Department, The University of Michigan.

Masters, Stanley. 1975. *Black–White Income Differentials*. New York: Academic Press.

Medoff, J., and K. Abraham. 1981. "Are Those Paid More Really More Productive? The Case of Experience." *Journal of Human Resources* 16:186–216.

Minarik, Joseph. 1975. "New Evidence on the Poverty Count." In American Statistical Association, *Proceedings of the Social Statistics Section*, 1975:544–559.

Mincer, Jacob. 1974. *Schooling, Experience, and Earnings*. New York: National Bureau of Economic Research.

———. 1978. "Family Migration Decisions." *Journal of Political Economy* 86:749–773.

Mincer, Jacob, and Haim Ofek. 1982. "Interrupted Work Careers." *Journal of Human Resources* 17:3–24.

Mincer, Jacob, and S. Polachek. 1974. "Family Investments in Human Capital: Earnings of Women." *Journal of Political Economy* Part II 82:576–608.

Morgan, James N. 1974. "Change in Global Measures." In *Five Thousand American Families—Patterns of Economic Progress*, Vol. 1, edited by James N. Morgan, et al. Ann Arbor: Institute for Social Research, The University of Michigan.

————. 1976. "A Seven Year Check on the Possible Effects of Attitudes, Motives, and Behavior Patterns on Change in Economic Status." In *Five Thousand American Families—Patterns of Economic Progress*, Vol. 4, edited by Greg J. Duncan and James N. Morgan, pp. 421–428. Ann Arbor: Institute for Social Research, The University of Michigan.

————. 1977. "Some Checks on the Representativeness of the Panel by Early 1975." In *Five Thousand American Families—Patterns of Economic Progress*, Vol. 5, edited by Greg J. Duncan and James N. Morgan. Ann Arbor: Institute for Social Research, The University of Michigan.

————. 1978. "Intra-Family Transfers Revisited: The Support of Dependents Inside the Family." In *Five Thousand American Families—Patterns of Economic Progress*, Vol. 6, edited by Greg J. Duncan and James N. Morgan. Ann Arbor: Institute for Social Research, The University of Michigan.

————. 1979. "Hours of Work by Family Heads: Constraints, Marginal Choices, and Income Goals." In *Five Thousand American Families—Patterns of Economic Progress*, Vol. 7, edited by Greg J. Duncan and James N. Morgan, pp. 63–100. Ann Arbor: Institute for Social Research, The University of Michigan.

Morgan, James N., Katherine Dickinson, Jonathan Dickinson, Jacob Benus, and Greg J. Duncan. 1974. *Five Thousand American Families—Patterns of Economic Progress*, Vol. 1, Ann Arbor: Institute for Social Research, The University of Michigan.

Oaxaca, Ronald. "Male–Female Wage Differentials in Urban Labor Markets." *International Economic Review* 14:693–709.

Orshansky, Mollie. 1969. "How Poverty is Measured." *Monthly Labor Review* 92:37–41.

Paglin, Morton. 1980. *Poverty and Transfers In-Kind*. Stanford, CA: Hoover Institution Press.

Pascal, Anthony, ed. 1972. *Racial Discrimination in Economic Life*. Lexington, MA: Lexington Books.

Rainwater, Lee. 1975. *What Money Buys: Inequality and the Social Meanings of Income*. New York: Basic Books.

————. 1980. "Persistent and Transitory Poverty: A New Look." Mimeographed. Cambridge, MA: Joint Center for Urban Studies.

Rein, Martin, and Lee Rainwater. 1978. "Patterns of Welfare Use." *Social Service Review* 52:511–534.

Rydell, D. Peter, et al. 1974. *Welfare Caseload Dynamics in New York City*. Santa Monica, CA: The Rand Corporation.

Sawhill, Isabel. 1973. "The Economics of Discrimination Against Women: Some New Findings." *The Journal of Human Resources* 8:386–387.

Schiller, Bradley R. 1976. *The Economics of Poverty and Discrimination*. 2nd ed. Englewood Cliffs, NJ: Prentice-Hall.

————. 1977. "Relative Earnings Mobility in the United States." *American Economic Review* 67:926–941.

Schultz, T.W. "Investment in Human Capital." *American Economic Review* 51:1–17.

Sheehan, Susan. 1976. *A Welfare Mother*. Boston: Houghton-Mifflin.

Smith, James P., and Finis Welch. 1978. "Race Differences in Earnings: A

Survey and New Evidence." R-229-NSF. Santa Monica, CA: The Rand Corporation.

Stafford, Frank P., and Greg J. Duncan. 1980. "The Use of Time and Technology by Households in the United States." In *Research in Labor Economics*, Vol. 3, edited by R.G. Ehrenberg. Greenwich, CT: JAI Press.

Townsend, Peter. 1979. *Poverty in the United Kingdom*. Harmondsworth, England: Penguin Book, Ltd.

U.S. Bureau of the Census. 1980. *Statistical Abstract of the United States: 1980*. 101st ed. Washington, D.C.: U.S. Government Printing Office.

U.S. Department of Health, Education, and Welfare. 1976. *The Measure of Poverty—A Report to Congress as Mandated by the Education Amendments of 1974*. Washington, D.C.: U.S. Department of Health, Education, and Welfare.

U.S. Department of Labor. 1973. *Manpower and Training Report of the President*. Washington, D.C.: U.S. Department of Labor.

Vickery, Clair. 1977. "The Time Poor: A New Look at Poverty." *Journal of Human Resources* 12:27–48.

Warlick, Jennifer. 1982. "Participation of the Aged in SSI." *Journal of Human Resources* 17:236–260.

Welch, Finis. 1973. "Black–White Differences in Returns to Schooling." *American Economic Review* 63:893–907.

Glossary–Index

ACHIEVEMENT MOTIVATION, **24–25, 59, 65, 70, 109–112.** Refers to a personality measure (from social psychology) showing the extent to which an individual derives satisfaction from overcoming obstacles by his or her own efforts in situations where the outcome is uncertain.

COHORT, **140–141.** A group of individuals sharing a common demographic characteristic, usually year of birth.

COHORT EFFECTS, **140–147.** Effects resulting from conditions related to the demographic characteristic that defines the cohort; for example, a year-of-birth cohort may show long-lasting effects of economic conditions prevailing when they were born, or effects of market discrimination that existed when they entered the labor market as young adults. Cohort effects are also sometimes referred to as "vintage" or "generation effects."

DUAL LABOR MARKET THEORY, **107–108, 114–115, 118, 121–122, 124, 136, 164–165.** An institutional view of the labor market in which jobs can be roughly classified as "good"—providing high pay, security, and ample promotion possibilities—or "bad"—lacking in these characteristics—with little movement between those two sectors.

EFFICACY, **24–25, 59, 65, 70, 109–112.** Refers to a personality measure showing the extent to which an individual perceives that his or her own individual plans and actions are effective. "Efficacy" is closely related to measures of "fate control" and "internal–external control."

FAMILY, **11–12, 17–24.** Defined as persons living together who are related by blood, marriage, adoption, or permanence of the living arrangement. The Panel Study considers unmarried persons living together for more than one year to belong to the same "family," while temporary "roommates," or persons keeping separate expenses, are not. In contrast to the Census Bureau's practice of classifying single persons as "unrelated individuals," the Panel Study considers them to be "families" consisting of a single member. The Panel Study also defines "household" as synonomous with "family."

FAMILY INCOME, 11–22, 28–29, 36. The sum of labor, capital, and transfer cash income of all family members. In-kind (e.g., food stamp) income is not included unless noted.

FUTURE ORIENTATION, 24–25, 59, 65, 70. A personality measure showing the extent to which an individual thinks about and plans for the future.

HEAD OF FAMILY—*see* HEAD OF HOUSEHOLD

HEAD OF HOUSEHOLD, 11, 97. In nuclear (husband–wife) families, for Panel Study purposes, the husband is arbitrarily designated the head of household (to conform to Census Bureau definitions in effect at the time the Panel Study began). (Note that this definition sometimes requires the use of the term "head of household *and wife*.") In families having only one adult, he or she is defined as the head. In non-nuclear families having more than one adult, the head is defined as the major earner or the one who owns the home or pays the rent. Note that the person designated as head of a Panel Study family may change over time as a result of other changes affecting that family.

HOUSEHOLD—*see* FAMILY

HUMAN CAPITAL, 47, 106–107, 109–112, 115, 121–124, 138, 155–164. The economically valued skills that result from investing in oneself—for example, through activities involving one's education, other training, health, or migration.

INCOME/NEEDS—*see* INCOME-TO-NEEDS

INCOME-TO-NEEDS, 11–22, 28–29, 55–60, 70. The ratio of total family income to a POVERTY NEED STANDARD based on family size and composition. If this ratio is unity (1), then the family's income places it just at the poverty line. If it is less than unity, then the family is deemed poor.

NEED STANDARD—*see* POVERTY NEED STANDARD

PERSISTENT POVERTY, 37–38, 41–42, 48–52, 60–65, 85–89. Defined as having family income below the POVERTY NEED STANDARD in at least eight years of a ten-year period.

PERSISTENT WELFARE DEPENDENT, 75–81, 89–92. Defined as receiving WELFARE INCOME amounting to more than half of the total income of the HEAD OF HOUSEHOLD and wife in at least eight years of a ten-year period.

PERSISTENT WELFARE RECEIPT, 75–81, 89–92. Defined as receiving any amount of WELFARE INCOME in at least eight years of a ten-year period. *See also* WELFARE DEPENDENT.

POVERTY, **33–65, 85–89.** Defined as having family income less than the POVERTY NEED STANDARD for that family. *See also* PERSISTENT POVERTY, TEMPORARY POVERTY.

POVERTY LINE—*see* POVERTY NEED STANDARD

POVERTY NEED STANDARD, **35–37, 42–43.** An estimate of the annual income necessary for a family to meet its basic needs; also referred to as the "poverty line." The Panel Study uses the method that is used to generate the official federal poverty line, which takes into account differences in family sizes and the sex and ages of family members.

QUINTILE, **12–14, 116–118.** If all units (e.g., all families, all individuals) are arranged in ascending order according to some criterion such as income and divided into five equal groups, the resulting five groups represent quintiles of the population on that criterion. *See also* VENTILE.

REGRESSION, **19, 55, 110, 161.** Refers to a statistical technique that is used to estimate the effect of a given measure on some criterion (dependent) measure net of the effect of the other measures included in the analysis. For example, the effect of educational level on income level, independent of IQ, motivation, or age.

SIGNIFICANT; SIGNIFICANCE. Refers to research findings that have met statistical tests for significance. Because Panel Study findings are based on a sample of the population and not (as is the dicennial census) on the entire population, it is important to be able to test whether a given effect found in the Panel Study sample is also likely to be found in the population as a whole. Tests of statistical inference can calculate the probability that a given effect does not exist in the population as a whole; if the calculated probability is five percent or less, the effect is considered statistically significant.

SPLITOFF, **11–12, 21, 82–83.** Refers to any individual who has moved away from his or her original Panel Study sample family and established a separate household. For example, adult children who leave home are splitoffs, and so is a divorced or separated spouse who establishes a new household while the other spouse (and perhaps children) remain in the original household.

STATISTICAL SIGNIFICANCE—*see* SIGNIFICANT; SIGNIFICANCE

TEMPORARY POVERTY, **37–38, 41–42, 48–52, 60–65, 85–89.** Defined as having family income below the POVERTY NEED STANDARD in only one or two years of a ten-year period.

TEMPORARY WELFARE, **75–81, 89–92.** Defined as receiving any WELFARE INCOME in only one or two years of a ten-year period.

TOTAL FAMILY INCOME—*see* FAMILY INCOME

TRANSFER INCOME, **9, 23, 71–92, 103–105.** Income from sources other than work or ownership of savings accounts or other capital assets. Private sources of transfer income include alimony, child support, and emergency help from friends or relatives; public sources include both contributory transfers (such as Social Security, unemployment compensation, and workers compensation, for which contributions are made), and noncontributory transfers (such as Aid to Families with Dependent Children and Supplemental Security Income).

VENTILE, **127.** If all units (e.g., all families, all individuals) are arranged in ascending order according to some criterion such as income and divided into 20 equal groups, the resulting 20 groups represent ventiles of the population on that criterion. *See also* QUINTILE.

VINTAGE EFFECT—*see* COHORT EFFECT

WELFARE DEPENDENT, **75–81, 89–92.** Defined as receiving WELFARE INCOME amounting to more than half of the total money income of the HEAD OF HOUSEHOLD and wife for a calendar year. *See also* PERSISTENT WELFARE DEPENDENT.

WELFARE INCOME, **71–92.** Defined as money income from the following public transfer income sources: Aid to Families with Dependent Children, General Assistance, and Supplemental Security Income. In-kind (e.g., food stamp) income is not included unless noted.

WELFARE RECEIPT, **71–92.** Defined as receiving any WELFARE INCOME.